OHIO HEISTS

HISTORIC BANK HOLDUPS, TRAIN ROBBERIES, JEWEL STINGS AND MORE

JANE ANN TURZILLO

THE
History
PRESS

Published by The History Press
Charleston, SC
www.historypress.com

Copyright © 2021 by Jane Ann Turzillo
All rights reserved

First published 2021

Manufactured in the United States

ISBN 9781467145565

Library of Congress Control Number: 2020951644

For my family, with all my love

I don't drink much and I smoke very little. I guess my only bad habit is robbing banks. Now you see, fellas, I ain't such a bad guy.

—John Dillinger

CONTENTS

ACKNOWLEDGEMENTS

Writing can be a lonely job, but not when the project is nonfiction history. It takes some curious librarians, generous historians, knowledgeable beta readers and a supportive family. In addition, it has been my pleasure to work with a great editor, John Rodrigue, for the second time.

Some of the people who helped with research and photos are friends, and some are folks who I met for the first time. Whether they knew me or not, they all wanted to help. Without them, this book would not have been possible. Many, many thanks to Mazie M. Adams, executive director, Cleveland Police Historical Society and Museum; Dale Albright, Norwalk Public Library; David Bailey, Toledo Police Museum; Christopher D. Barth, associate dean and director of libraries and archives, United States Military Academy; Devin Bean, student manager, archives and special collections, Kenyon College; Cleo Bell, senior library services assistant, Genealogy & Local History Department, Public Library of Cincinnati and Hamilton County; Robert J. Cermak, retired commander, Cleveland Police, Cleveland Police Museum; Judith G. Cetina, PhD, Cuyahoga County Archives; James Dailey II, author; Alan Dutka, author; Pete Elliott, U.S. marshal, Northern District of Ohio; John K. Elliott, retired deputy U.S. marshal; Shirley Green, Toledo Police Museum; Caryn Hilfer, executive administrator, *Cleveland Plain Dealer*; Karen Huck, Montano Historical Society; Wendy Koile, author; Irv Korman, author; Rebecca Larson-Troyer, Akron-Summit County Public Library; Lyndsey, Akron-Summit County Public Library; Brian Meggitt, Photography Collection librarian, Cleveland

Public Library; Russell Metcalf; Vern Morrison, Digital Production Unit coordinator, Michael Schwartz Library, Cleveland State University; Carrie Phillips, Bluffton University, Musselman Library; Michael D. Pittman, photographer; Russ Rattray, associate professor, associate library director, H. Raymond Danforth Library (Henniker, New Hampshire); James Renner, author; Abigail Tayse, College & Digital Collections archivist, Kenyon College; and Beth Thieman, Toledo Police Department.

I have my brainstorming group to thank for support and therapy. They are Julie Anne Lindsey, Kathryn Long, Cari Dubiel, Wendy Campbell and Shellie Arnold.

A special thanks to my beta readers, Marilyn Seguin, and my sister, Mary Turzillo, PhD. This is the eighth book they've critiqued for me.

This book was also made possible by those period journalists whose bylines never appeared at the tops of their stories.

And finally, I want to thank my son, John-Paul Paxton, and my grandsons, Nicholas and Nathan, for their love and encouragement. I am also thankful for the company of my beagle, Wyatt Earp, who lies under my desk while I write, and my German shepherd, Doc Holliday, who is too big to get under my desk, but lies beside my chair.

I hope I have not forgotten anyone. If I have, it was not intentional.

INTRODUCTION

On New Year's Day in 2004, I was watching television as I took down the Christmas tree and put away the trimmings. A jewel thief named Bill Mason was being interviewed on *Court TV*. He was handsome, charming and articulate. Since his crimes were all outside of the statute of limitations, he had authored a book detailing his prolific capers, for most of which he had never been held to account. He had worked as a cat burglar, stealing from the rich and famous in Fort Lauderdale and Pompano Beach, Florida. I knew those towns. They were part of my childhood and teen years. What most interested me was that he started and ended his criminal career around Cleveland. I got my hands on the book, made some notes and tucked the story away, knowing that someday I had to write about him. It was the beginning of my collecting stories of robbers and burglars.

Ted Conrad, a young man from Cleveland, walked away from the bank where he worked with a fifth of Canadian Club, a carton of Marlboros and $215,000 in a paper sack. No one was the wiser for three or four days. Apparently, Ted had been planning the embezzlement for some time. He got the idea from the movie *The Thomas Crown Affair*. He even began to dress and act like Steve McQueen. Ted had a high IQ and wanted to see if he could get away with it. He did get away with it. I added his story to my files.

I learned about a rare book thief from a fellow conference goer at Malice Domestic 2019. I came home and started to research his crimes. I had read about book thieves before, but until I followed David Breithaupt's story of looting the Kenyon College library of rare books and documents, I did not know how lucrative that crime could be.

"Cowboy" Hill, who had so many aliases that he may have forgotten he was really Joseph Muzzio, was the first robber to use "machines" (cars) to escape police. He turned up in a historical newspaper. I slid that old clipping into my thickening folder.

Photos from the Cleveland Police Museum showing the first camera installed in a bank piqued my curiosity. The camera led to the arrest of Steven Ray Thomas and his two teenage female accomplices.

Resurrection men were in the business of body snatching. They robbed graves and sold the bodies to medical colleges for research. They ran into grave trouble when they robbed John Scott Harrison's tomb. He was both the son and the father of U.S. presidents.

Some of the deadliest and most flamboyant robbers of the Depression era were John Dillinger, Charles Arthur "Pretty Boy" Floyd and Alvin Karpis. How could I not include them? It is hard to separate truth from legend with these bandits, but for sure Ohio was a favorite haunt for all three. They crisscrossed the state robbing banks and swapping lead with police.

Adrenaline ran high with all the criminals in this book. Some trusted firepower and fast cars to steal what they wanted and to get away with it. Others relied on their intelligence and cunning. All of these crooks depended on luck. For all but one, luck ran out.

1
THE PEOPLE'S BANDIT

John Herbert Dillinger was a folk hero to those who had been hit hardest by the Great Depression. They saw him as a sort of Robin Hood who had nerve and style while robbing the banks that had robbed them of their jobs and homes. Some called him the people's bandit. He held a grip on the public's imagination as his crimes dominated the front pages of nearly every newspaper in the country.

Dillinger's thirteen and a half months of infamy ran from his first bank job in New Carlisle, Ohio, on June 21, 1933, to his violent death in Chicago on July 22, 1934. It included a string of bank and police arsenal robberies, three dramatic jail breaks and gun battles throughout the Midwest. He wielded a stolen Thompson submachine gun and wore a purloined bulletproof vest. His trademark was vaulting over bank counters. Either he or a member of his gang was responsible for the deaths of ten men, including a sheriff, and the wounding of seven others.

It began on May 22, 1933, after Johnnie, as he was known to friends and family, was freshly paroled after doing eight and a half years at the Indiana State Prison in Michigan City for a botched 1924 grocery store robbery. When Dillinger came home to his father's farm in Mooresville, Indiana, he found his wife had divorced him, and his stepmother, whom he had grown to love, had died only hours before.

He looked for work, but times were tough and there was none—especially not for an ex-con. He helped his father on the farm for a while, but after a few weeks, he grew restless and started looking for something else.

John Dillinger robbed banks in New Carlisle, Bluffton and Fostoria. *Author's collection.*

According to FBI files, Dillinger was embittered and resentful for having to serve such a harsh sentence. At the time, his father, John W., advised him to own up to his wrongdoing and plead guilty. His father thought that would ensure a light sentence. It did not work. The judge sentenced him to ten to twenty. By contrast, Edgar Singleton, who had put young Johnnie up to the grocery store robbery, hired a lawyer, pleaded not guilty, went to trial and received a much lighter sentence.

During his time at the Michigan City prison, Dillinger aligned himself with some of the worst crooks of the day and obtained a solid education in crime. What he learned from the likes of Harry "Handsome Harry" (a.k.a. "Pete") Pierpont, Charles "Fat Charley" Makley, Russell Clark, Edward Shouse, Walter Dietrich, John Burns, James Jenkins, Joseph Fox, John "Red" Hamilton and James "Oklahoma Jack" Clark started him on the road to becoming the most famous bank robber of the twentieth century.

Dillinger picked the New Carlisle (Ohio) National Bank at the southeast corner of Main and Jefferson Streets for his first bank job. On the recommendation of Pierpont, Dillinger lined up Paul "Lefty" Parker, Noble Claycomb and William Shaw to help him rob the bank, according to an excerpt from Bill Berry in the *New Carlisle News*. All three, members of the White Cap Gang, were experienced in small-time robberies.

Dillinger had heard—probably from Pierpont—that a bathroom window at the back of the New Carlisle National Bank building was always left open even when the bank was closed. On Tuesday, June 20, 1933, the four men climbed into a new Ford vehicle in Indianapolis and headed for the bank in New Carlisle.

They rolled into town after dark and drove around back of the small bank. The tip was solid. The window next to the toilet was open. They parked the car on Jefferson Street two blocks west of the bank. Leaving Claycomb behind the wheel, Dillinger, Shaw and Parker slid through the open window and waited for the bank to open and the time lock on the vault to expire in the morning.

Shortly after eight o'clock the next morning, bookkeeper Horace Grisso unlocked the bank's door. He stepped into the lobby and rolled up the blinds on the windows. As he turned, he came face to face with three masked men stepping out from behind the counter. They were aiming guns at him. "Keep still and obey orders," one of them said, according to the *Dayton Daily News*. Grisso said the leader—most likely Dillinger—ordered him to "Open the safe or we'll blow your head off." Grisso proceeded to the vault, which was right behind the counter and in plain view of the windows. Unfortunately, the action drew no attention from the outdoors.

Grisso was purposely slow to work the combination. Realizing Grisso was stalling, one of the bandits threatened him. "Open the inner compartment of this safe, and do it in a hurry or you'll get yours," an article in the paper reported.

"I'm a new clerk here and don't know much about this safe." Grisso claimed, hoping cashier Carl Enochs would arrive soon.

But instead, assistant cashier Mata Taylor was next on the scene. The crooks hid until she was inside. Nothing seemed awry to her until she walked toward the counter. One of the robbers then jumped out from his hiding place. Pointing his gun at her, he demanded she open the cash drawer in the vault. Terrified, she told them she did not have access.

The bandits forced Grisso and Taylor to stretch out face-down on the floor behind the counter. Taylor's green smock lay on the counter. "Lie down on the floor and keep calm." One of the bandits—most likely Dillinger—noticed it and told her to spread it out on the floor before lying down. After the robbers bound her and Grisso's arms and legs with wire, they quickly scooped up the coins and poured them into a bag they had brought with them. They gagged the pair on the floor and took up their positions behind the counter to await the next employee who they hoped could open the vault.

Cashier Enochs anticipated the bank's front door would already be open. He found it was locked, so he used his own keys and went inside. Dillinger, Shaw and Parker sprang from behind the counter with guns in hand. They ordered him to open up the cash drawer in the vault. Enochs tried to delay, but their threats hurried him along.

Once the drawer was open, they bound and gagged Enochs. They quickly gathered up the folding money and stashed it in the same bag as the coins, then raced out the rear door and piled into their waiting car and sped east on Route 71 (now 571). In what would become one of Dillinger's signature moves, they scattered a keg of roofing nails for about a mile behind them to discourage pursuit.

Martha Weeks, who lived next door to the bank, saw the men running through her yard. Suspecting something was wrong at the bank, she got on the phone to the authorities.

Enochs described the bandits to Clark County sheriff George Benham and Springfield chief George Abele. He said they were masked, but he thought they were about thirty years old. They were a "hardboiled" type, he told them. Police showed photos of known robbers to the bank employees, but they were unable to identify any of them.

Dillinger and his pals had come away with $10,600, a surprisingly large amount of money for a small bank during the Depression. Dillinger planned on using some of the money to buy guns to smuggle to his pals who were still behind the walls of the Michigan City Prison.

That same evening, Dillinger, Shaw and Parker returned to Indianapolis and hit a drugstore and supermarket. The haul between the two was $3,600. At least four more Indiana and Kentucky bank jobs followed.

Dillinger returned to doing business with Ohio banks in August. The Bluffton Citizen's Bank on South Main and Church Streets was his target on Monday, August 14, 1933. He and his buddies (one possibly being Sam Goldstein) parked their green sedan with Indiana plates facing west on Church Street near the bank and left a driver behind the wheel and the car motor rumbling.

Ken Hauenstein, who was eight at the time of the robbery, remembered seeing the car parked with all four doors wide open. According to a 2017 Associated Press story, he saw a man pacing up and down the street and looking around the corners every so often.

Dillinger robbed the Bluffton Citizen's Bank on August 14, 1933. *Bluffton University Library.*

The most complete account of the robbery came from *Bluffton News* editor Clarence A. Biery, who witnessed the holdup. He wrote about the theft in the newspaper a few days after the robbery. The article is now in the digital collection of Ohio Memory.

At 11:55 a.m., it was business as usual at the bank. Cashier Elmer C. Romey was waiting on Charles Burkholder at the first window, closest to the street. Burkholder was the only customer in the bank at the time. Assistant teller Roscoe Klinger was at the third window, the farthest from the street.

Three strange men, who looked to be in their thirties, entered the bank. All three were well dressed, two of them in light gray suits and straw hats, the third wearing a blue suit. None wore masks. The blue-suited man stayed close to the door. One of the others, most likely Dillinger, strolled to a glass-top table opposite the second window and leaned on it. The third man went to the third window, farthest from the street, and asked Klinger to change a five-dollar bill. He wanted three one-dollar bills, a dollar in nickels and a dollar in dimes. Once he had pocketed the change, he pulled a gun and pointed it at Klinger. "Stand back. This is a hold up." He drew a second gun and pointed it at Buckholder, who was moving closer.

At that, five-foot, seven-inch, 153-pound Dillinger swiftly leaped over the cashier's counter with the agility of a wildcat. "Hands up," he said to Romey and a third employee, Oliver Locher. He shoved the money on the counter into a canvas bag then grabbed Locher. "You've got more money than that around here," Dillinger accused. "Where is it?"

Klinger, Romey, Locher and Burkholder were lying face-down on the floor with the two-gun bandit holding both weapons on them. Locher told Dillinger the money was in the time-locked safe as a precaution against robbery.

Just then, the bank alarm shrieked. The robber with the weapons got nervous. "They're after us. Let's go." But Dillinger held his cool and searched the counter and tellers' drawers for more money. He found a .32-caliber gun on the cashier's counter and pocketed it.

Both the two-gun robber and the blue-suited bandit near the door ran from the bank. Holding guns in both hands, the men took up a position at the street corner, guarding the approach to the bank with a hail of .45-caliber bullets. A fourth bandit in shirtsleeves appeared from the corner waving a machine gun.

Dillinger finally ran outside and, under cover of gunfire, made his way to the waiting car. The other three men followed. They dove into the car. As they sped away, one of the robbers kept the machine gun pointed out the window in case someone tried to follow. The car roared down Church Street and then turned north on Jackson.

The filling station attendant, Harold Montgomery, saw the car coming north on Jackson. He said it skidded when the driver applied its brakes to turn onto Riley. It slowed down for the intersection, then shot north.

Although witnesses all agreed on the color of the car, there were varying opinions about the make. Some thought it was a Chevrolet or a Buick, while someone else thought it was a Pontiac, or possibly an Essex. For certain it had an Indiana license plate, but the plate was dirty and unreadable.

The gunfire left several windows shattered and a variety of other damage up and down the street. Copper-jacketed and soft-nosed bullets were the only shells found on the sidewalk, so it was unlikely the machine gun had been fired. No one was hurt.

According to a Bluffton Police Department's modern-day website, the robbery took less than five minutes. The amount of the take is up for dispute. Several sources claim it was only $2,100, but the bank's website has it at $6,000.

While incarcerated in Indiana, Dillinger had promised some of his fellow inmates that he would call on their families when he got out on parole. One of those inmates, James Jenkins, had a sister named Mary Jenkins Longnaker who lived in Dayton. Dillinger was captivated by the attractive twenty-two-year-old divorcée with two children, and Mary fell for "Johnnie." He was handsome, with gray eyes, brown hair and a slight scar over his lip. He had a quick wit, dressed well and always had money. He took her on trips, including to the World's Fair in Chicago and to meet his family in Mooresville. He visited her often at her rooming house in Dayton.

By September 1933, Dillinger and his pals had committed six robberies in Ohio and Indiana and escaped with at least $50,000. According to Elliot J. Gorn in *Dillinger's Wild Ride*, Dillinger's Indiana parole officer, Frank Hope; retired Pinkerton detective Forrest Huntington; and Matt Leach of the Indiana State Police were hot on his trail.

According to author John Toland in *Dillinger Days*, Huntington learned about Mary Longnaker from either ex-con informant Arthur McGinnis or former Dillinger associate Clifford "Whitey" Mohler. Huntington turned over the information to the Pinkerton Detective Agency. Having been hired to crack the Bluffton heist, Pinkerton took the information to Dayton police inspector Seymour E. Yendes. It also came to light that Dillinger was driving a new Essex Terraplane S black sedan. Yendes assigned Detective Sergeants Russell Pfauhl and Charles Gross to keep an eye out on Mary's

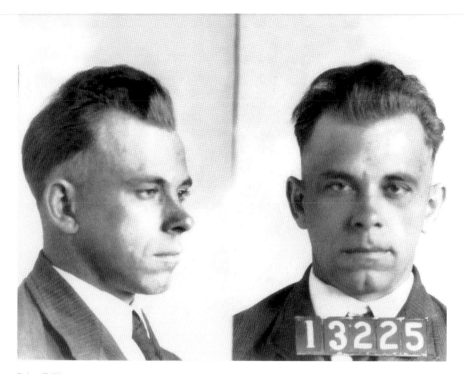

John Dillinger mug shot from the Indiana State Prison. *Author's collection.*

boardinghouse at 324 West First Avenue. The two detectives paid a visit to Mary's landlady, Lucille Stricker, and showed her a photo of Dillinger. Stricker identified him as the man who visited Mary and also wrote to her quite often. A few days after the meeting with the detectives, a letter came addressed to Mary from Dillinger. Instead of giving it to Mary, Stricker handed it over to Pfauhl and Gross. Dillinger wrote that he would be seeing Mary soon, but he gave no definite date.

Figuring Dillinger would appear sooner rather than later, the detectives sat on the house and waited. After several weeks, he was a no-show, so they left. Finally, Stricker called and told them Dillinger was in Mary's apartment.

At 1:30 a.m. on September 22, police quietly surrounded the house. Pfauhl, Gross and Sergeant William J. Aldredge went into the house with a sawed-off shotgun and machine gun. While Aldredge stayed at the bottom of the stairs to block an escape attempt, Pfauhl and Gross climbed to the second-floor apartment of Mary Longnaker. Stricker was told to knock on the door. When Mary answered, the landlady stepped aside. Dillinger was standing up looking at some pictures from the World's Fair. When he saw the lawmen and their firepower, he dropped the pictures and slowly raised his hands.

Mary tried to pull a distraction by fainting, but it did not work. Dillinger surrendered peacefully and was arrested.

Police searched Dillinger's possessions and found five pistols, $2,604 in cash, two suitcases full of ammunition and maps showing the fastest routes out of several Indiana cities. He had boxes of roofing tacks, which he and his gang used to dump on the roads to hinder pursuit. When they frisked him, they found a plan for a prison break.

Indiana State Police captain Matt Leach was eager to get his hands on Dillinger for four Indiana bank jobs. Indiana governor Paul McNutt rescinded Dillinger's clemency order and wanted him back in the state slammer. Ohio authorities wanted to keep him to stand trial for the Bluffton robbery. During questioning by police agencies, Dillinger remained cool and kept a smirk on his face. "See my lawyer," he said when asked questions.

Dillinger did not want to face the music in Indiana and possibly go back to Michigan City, so he hired attorney Jack Egan, who advised him to plead guilty to the Bluffton robbery. Dillinger took that advice, and Common Pleas judge Robert C. Patterson turned Dillinger over to Allen County authorities, who put him in jail in Lima.

On September 26, just four days after Dillinger's arrest, eight of his Michigan City prison buddies escaped from jail. Using four pistols and ammunition Dillinger had smuggled into the jail's shirt factory inside a crate of thread, the prisoners overpowered the guards to get away.

Leach claimed papers, including maps and letters found on Dillinger at his arrest in Dayton, could have prevented the jailbreak, but Dayton authorities did not turn them over to him.

While Dillinger sat in jail in Lima, five or six of the Michigan City escapees headed to St. Mary's, Ohio, on Tuesday, October 3 to rob the First National Bank. They chose St. Mary's because one of the gang, Charles "Fat Charlie" Makley, was from there and likely knew the lay of the land. They hit the bank around three o'clock in the afternoon and grabbed $10,000—enough to fund another jail break, this time for Dillinger.

There are varying accounts of Dillinger's jailbreak in Lima. They come from newspapers, books and the FBI.

What is basically known is that the Allen County sheriff Jess L. Sarber was not worried that the Michigan City escapees might come for Dillinger, so security was lax. Before his tenure as sheriff, Sarber owned a used car business. It had failed during the Depression, so he ran for sheriff.

Around 6:30 p.m. on October 12, 1933, Harry Copeland, John "Red" Hamilton and Edward Shouse waited in two cars outside the jail while Harry Pierpont, "Fat Charlie" Makley and Russell Clark went inside.

Sarber and his wife, Lucy, had just finished supper of pork chops and mashed potatoes. The forty-seven-year-old sheriff was at his desk reading the *Lima News*. His wife sat across from him working a crossword puzzle. Deputy Wilbert Sharpe was napping on a couch nearby. Neither police officer wore his gun. Sarber's gun was in his desk drawer, and Sharpe's belt and gun were lying within reach on the desktop.

Pierpont, Clark and Makley presented themselves as officers from Michigan City. "We want to see John Dillinger," one of them said.

"Let me see your credentials," Sarber replied.

Pierpont pulled a gun from the pocket of his coat and aimed it at Sarber. "Here are my credentials."

Some accounts say Sarber started to move toward the gun on his desk and Pierpont shot him. Other accounts say Pierpont pulled the trigger twice with no provocation. One of the bullets tore into the sheriff's abdomen, and he sank to the floor.

The bandits turned their attention to Sharpe and demanded the keys. When

No. 183, Harry Pierpont
of Allen County, Electrocuted October 17th, 1934, for the Murder of Sheriff Jesse Sarber.

Harry Pierpont died in the electric chair for murdering Allen County sheriff Jess L. Sarber. *Ohio History Connection.*

Sharpe claimed he did not have them, Markley yelled at the prostrate Sarber and told him to hand over the keys. Sarber was trying to rise, but Markley struck the sheriff in the head with the butt of his gun.

"Please don't hurt him anymore!" Lucy Sarber screamed and quickly handed over the keys.

Dillinger, who had been playing cards in the bullpen, heard the commotion and grabbed his hat and coat. The crooks locked Deputy Sharpe and Lucy Sarber in the jail and dashed out the door, leaving Sarber to die on the floor by his desk.

They joined Copeland, Shouse and Hamilton outside the jail, jumped into two waiting cars and fled toward Hamilton.

Dillinger and his gang crisscrossed Indiana, Illinois and Wisconsin robbing banks and police arsenals, where they stole guns and bulletproof vests. They took hostages and got into gun battles in which they wounded or killed police officers and others. They were captured in Tucson, Arizona, on January 25, 1934. Pierpont, Makley and Clark were sent back to Ohio to stand trial for Sheriff Sarber's murder. With the help of former gang member Edward Shouse's testimony against them, they were found guilty. Pierpont and Makley were sentenced to die. Clark was given life.

Dillinger was taken back to jail in Crown Point, Indiana, to stand trial for the death of a police officer during an East Chicago bank robbery. He broke out of the Crown Point jail using a wooden gun he had carved out of a washboard brace with a razor.

After that, Dillinger broadened the field by holding up banks in South Dakota, Iowa and Minnesota. Both he and John "Red" Hamilton were wounded during the Iowa robbery. He went home to Mooresville to recuperate.

The gang's most famous escape was at the Little Bohemia Lodge in Wisconsin, where they got away unharmed. A federal agent died, two officers were wounded and three bystanders were shot, one fatally, by FBI agents. Dillinger, Homer Van Meter and Hamilton headed for St. Paul but got into another gun battle with local police. Hamilton was wounded a second time and died four days later. Dillinger got away unscathed.

Dillinger and Van Meter came back to Ohio to rob the First National Bank of Fostoria on May 3, 1934. They double parked their car across from the bank. With their machine guns hidden under their topcoats, they walked into the bank. "Stick 'em up," one of them said. "There won't be any shooting as long as you do as you're told."

Inside the bank, the robbers pressed for the money from the vault, then demanded, "Give us the bond box." Andrew Emerline, president of the bank, gave them a box with bonds valued at a few hundred dollars instead of the one holding more than $80,000.

Fostoria police chief Frank Culp happened to be across the street and saw what was going down. He ordered one of his officers to run to the station for more men and a machine gun. He went into the bank alone to face the robbers with only his pistol. One of the gunmen saw Culp's uniform, panicked, and shot him. The chief was felled with a bullet in his lungs.

By this time, a crowd had gathered outside the bank. To keep everyone back, one of the bandits let loose with a barrage of machine gun fire through the bank's front window, spraying glass shards all over the street and lobby. The other robber hurriedly snatched up the rest of the money.

Above: A courtroom scene from one of Dillinger's trials. *Author's collection.*

Right: Believed to be Dillinger's gun. *Butler County Ohio Sheriff's Office. Photo by Michael D. Pittman.*

Escape was no small feat. More police had arrived. The officers and five armed citizens began firing at the outlaws. The robbers herded bank employees William J. Daub, Ruth Harris, Ralph Barbour and Harold Lusky through the door to use as human shields, all the while unleashing a torrent of machine gun fire in order to get to their car.

Despite being wounded, Culp dragged himself into the line of fire and emptied his gun of bullets. None hit the robbers.

Two of their hostages, Harris and Daub, were forced to stand on the running boards as the car pulled away from the bank. One of the robbers drove as the other aimed his machine gun out the back window. They spread roofing tacks behind them as they headed toward Toledo. Harris and Daub were released unharmed two miles out of town. The loot amounted to $17,299.

Five people were injured in the fray. Besides Culp, a sixty-seven-year-old farmer, William Feasel, had been hit in the chest and was in serious condition. Bank cashier Ralph S. Powley received a flesh wound when a bullet glanced off his suspender button. Edward Walters, a former city patrolman, and William Shields, a carpenter, both received minor leg wounds. All the victims, including Culp, recovered.

The Findley police radio blasted the news along with descriptions of the robbers and their car. The Columbus station picked up the transmission and spread it throughout northern Ohio. The northern section of the state was alive with police presence, but the bandits eluded them.

Ralph Barbour, who had been used as a shield, was certain one of the men was John Dillinger, but authorities doubted him. He and Harris described one of the men as having red hair, wearing glasses and being about thirty-five years old. They said he was about five feet, eight inches and weighed in the neighborhood of 150 pounds. He wore a light-colored suit. They described the other man as having a dark complexion and weighing 170 pounds. He wore a dark suit and was also about thirty-five.

While thousands of police and federal agents combed the roads of northern Ohio and Indiana, two federal and private investigators inspected the bank for clues. They paid the most attention to smudgy fingerprints on one of the cash drawers. Days later, H.C. Robinson from the State Bureau of Identification determined the prints did not belong to Dillinger or any of his gang. This led police to wonder if Dillinger had a new recruit they did not know about.

Justice officials from Detroit, which covered that area of Ohio, refused to investigate the Fostoria robbery because they were under the impression it was "pretty definitely established that Dillinger himself was not involved in the Fostoria case." Some authorities speculated that the robbery had been the work of a Michigan gang.

"It was him without any question," Barbour insisted, "only he wore no moustache."

"I can't be positive, but I noticed the peculiar expression of his mouth," Harris said. "And I think it was Dillinger."

Melvin Purvis, agent in charge of the Chicago office of the FBI at the time of Dillinger's death. *Author's collection.*

Fostoria patrolman Ross Staegger positively identified Homer Van Meter from a picture. Two days after the robbery, Toledo detectives had credible information that the machine gunner was indeed Homer Van Meter. They also developed information that led them to believe Dillinger was in Fostoria at the time of the robbery. By examining the gun shells from the scene, they could tell that more than two machine guns had been fired. Police wondered if a second carload of gangsters was close by as backup for the men in the bank. They theorized the second car fled the scene to confuse pursuers.

Dillinger remained free for two and a half more months. During that time, he was implicated in the death of two East Chicago police officers. He also had plastic surgery to build up his nose, fill in the dimple in his chin and tighten the skin on his face. On his thirty-first birthday, he was declared Public Enemy Number One. That day, he and his gang robbed the Merchant's National Bank in South Bend, Indiana, where one policeman was killed and several citizens were wounded. The take was $30,000.

Finally, on July 22, 1934, John Dillinger was gunned down by FBI agents led by Melvin Purvis outside the Biograph Theater in Chicago.

2
THE CONRAD CAPER

By all accounts, twenty-year-old Theodore John Conrad was a model employee at the Society National Bank headquarters on Public Square in Cleveland. By July 1969, young Ted had worked for seven months as a vault teller, packaging money to send out to branch banks. He was hired with excellent references. Bank officials and fellow employees thought highly of him, and his performance reviews reflected that. He was a charming, smart, handsome young man, blond, blue-eyed, six feet tall with an engaging smile. Everyone who knew him—from high school classmates to bank co-workers—said had a bright future and was headed for the fast track.

But Ted's idea of a bright future and the fast track was quite different than theirs.

During his lunch hour on Friday, July 11, 1969 (one day after his twentieth birthday), Ted walked a block down the street to a liquor store and bought a fifth of Canadian Club and a carton of Marlboro cigarettes. He took his purchase back to the bank in a brown paper sack. After lunch with a friend, he made a point of showing security and co-workers the contents of the bag, informing them that he was going to party that weekend to celebrate his birthday.

At closing time, Ted told his vault partner to go ahead on out and he would be right along. His boss was in the hospital for surgery, so Ted was left in the vault by himself. Upon leaving the bank, he stopped and talked to the vice president of operations for twenty minutes, then smiled and waved at security and walked out of the bank carrying his sack of Canadian Club

Society National Bank where Ted Conrad was a vault teller. *Cleveland Press Collection, Cleveland State Library.*

and Marlboros. No one suspected that tucked in the bottom of the bag were $50 and $100 bills totaling $215,000. Adjusted for inflation, that sum would roughly equal $1.4 million in today's dollars.

Ted went home to his apartment on Clifton Boulevard and packed one small suitcase. Leaving his car behind, he climbed into a cab at 7:26 p.m.

Left: Theodore John Conrad. *Cleveland State Library and U.S. Marshals Service, Cleveland Office.*

Below: Society National Bank in downtown Cleveland. *Cleveland Public Library.*

MAIN BANKING ROOM
SOCIETY FOR SAVINGS
CLEVELAND

Above: Main banking room of Society National Bank. *Allen Dutka's collection.*

Right: Street view of Society National Bank. *Cleveland Public Library.*

and waved to his landlady as he left. Twenty-six minutes later, he was at Cleveland Hopkins Airport. Before he boarded a plane, he called his girlfriend, Kathleen Einhouse, and told her he was on his way to a rock concert in Erie, Pennsylvania.

The following Monday, Ted was absent from work. He did not call in—highly unusual for the punctual young man, who never missed a day. Co-workers were stumped and tried to call him, but they got no answer. Then they counted the money in the vault and found a substantial amount missing. Bank administrators did not call the FBI until the next day, and the story did not land in the papers until the day after that.

Up until that time, Ted had led the life of an ordinary twenty-year-old. His father, Edward E. Conrad, a captain in the navy, had moved his family several times. Ted was born in Denver. He had an older sister and younger brother. His parents divorced while he was in grade school. His mother, Ruthabeth, moved the children to Lakewood, where she married Raymond Marsh, who had two sons. Marsh owned a bar and bowling alley, according to Ted's best friend, Russell "Rusty" Metcalf.

There was friction between Ted and his stepfather, Metcalf said. Retired deputy U.S. marshal John K. Elliott, who worked the case in the beginning, noted, "He didn't get along with his stepfather, which may have been one of the reasons he left."

With an IQ of 135, Ted made excellent grades at Lakewood High School. He was popular with the student body and was voted onto student council. He joined the German Club but failed to have his senior picture taken for the yearbook. It was well known that he spoke fluent French. Metcalf said Ted and his mother would speak French with each other often.

Metcalf was with Ted the night before he left, and they had had lunch together on that Friday. Metcalf said Ted paid for lunch, which was unusual. When they parted after lunch, Ted hugged Metcalf and said, "I'll see you sometime." Metcalf thought that was a strange thing for his friend to say.

That evening, Metcalf went over to Ted's apartment, but Ted was not home. Figuring Ted had gone out for the night, Metcalf did not think too much about it, as they had plans to play golf the next day, Saturday. But Saturday came and went, and Metcalf did not hear from his friend.

Metcalf and Ted first met in 1965 and became close friends over the next two years. "He rode with me to high school. We played football. We double dated," Metcalf said.

After graduation from Lakewood High School in 1967, they both went away, Metcalf to the service and Ted to the New England College, a liberal arts college in Henniker, New Hampshire, where his father, who had retired from the navy, taught political science. Although Ted was elected president of the freshman class, he did not stay. After one semester, he came back to Lakewood and enrolled at Cuyahoga Community College. Metcalf thought it was because he had not gotten along with his father.

When Ted and Metcalf both got back to Lakewood, they picked up their friendship as if no time had passed. "He was fun," Metcalf said. "He was the closest male friend I had."

Metcalf went on to say that his whole family loved Ted. He recalled one July 4 when a tornado touched down close by. Ted came to Metcalf's house to make sure everyone was safe. Upon hearing Metcalf's brothers were not home, Ted went searching for them. "He was like that." Metcalf recalled Ted was truly concerned for his brothers. "He cared about other people."

In June 1968, *The Thomas Crown Affair*, a heist movie starring Steve McQueen, hit the theaters. It tells the story of a bored multimillionaire who pulls off the perfect crime by engineering the theft of $2.6 million from a Boston bank. It is all about deception, a game pitting Crown's cunning against investigators. That resonated with Ted.

Friends remembered Ted was fascinated with the movie. "He watched it over and over," Metcalf said. Ted was obsessed with Thomas Crown and began to emulate him. Ted not only dressed the part, but he also showed off his fluent French. He developed an interest in sports cars (especially Porsches) and drove a two-seater MG. A left-handed player, Ted became tournament proficient at billiards, Metcalf remembered.

According to a 1986 *Live On 5* news story with reporter Bill McKay, there was nothing in Ted's background—with the exception of minor shoplifting scrapes—to suggest he would go so far as to orchestrate a bank heist. But during that same news story, FBI special agent Bill Hahn told McKay that Ted had talked with friends about pulling off a heist. "It was a challenge to him."

According to a January 2008 *Plain Dealer* article by Jim Nichols, Ted even joked about how vulnerable the bank was. "Ted talked about how loose security was at the bank," Metcalf remembered. Looking back and taking everything into consideration, Metcalf was not too surprised at what Ted did. "I think he wanted to prove he could do it."

"The U.S. Marshals became involved right after it happened," said the now retired John K. Elliott, who was in his twenties when he was assigned to the case. Right from the beginning, he knew it was not going to be easy because the bank had no fingerprinting policy. Ted was bonded but never

One of the few photos of twenty-year-old Ted Conrad. *Cleveland Press Collection, CSU, Michael Schwartz Library and U.S. Marshals Service, Cleveland Office.*

fingerprinted. Ted had no criminal record to pull from. All Elliott had to start with was one photograph, but he was able to pull fingerprints from Ted's apartment, as well as documents that Ted had handled at the bank and his high school. Elliott then turned a dossier over to Interpol.

The FBI took boxes of evidence out of Ted's apartment, including a money bag from the bank and the bottle of Canadian Club. The bureau knows that he went from Cleveland to Washington, D.C., because his girlfriend, Kathleen, received a letter postmarked from Reagan International Airport on July 17. Five days later, she got a second letter. This letter was postmarked from Englewood, California, where the Los Angeles International Airport is located. In both letters, he admitted to taking the money. One of his letters wound up in the hands of the FBI. In it, Ted asked Kathleen to burn the envelopes "so the authorities don't get the postmarks." In another letter, Ted claimed to have drastically changed his appearance.

McKay's *Live On 5* report revealed that Ted had also telephoned Kathleen, and the FBI had a tape of that call. Part of it can be heard on McKay's report. Investigative reporter James Renner transcribed part of that conversation in a chapter on Ted Conrad included in his book *The Serial Killer's Apprentice*. Ted asked Kathleen if she had played her Beach Boys album. Kathleen apparently had friends there when he called, and he said, "Oh, I'm keeping you from your friends." She replied, "It's okay. It's my turn." Some of the call was inaudible.

Renner contacted Kathleen prior to the 2008 publication of his book. She told him one of Ted's letters referred to the statute of limitations as being seven years. What Ted did not know was that he had been indicted for embezzlement and falsifying bank records—crimes that carried a total of twenty years behind bars. That indictment stopped the clock on the statute of limitations.

Ted stopped contacting Kathleen in the fall. He never contacted his family. Ted's mother and grandmother thought someone put him up to the theft. Edward Conrad called his son's actions "the heartbreak of my life."

Metcalf never heard from Ted again, either. "He left a lot of good friends behind," Metcalf said wistfully.

In October 1969, a Beachwood couple on vacation in Waikiki happened to strike up a conversation over drinks with a young man at the bar in the Princess Kaiulani Hotel. The encounter lasted only about fifteen minutes, but during the conversation the young man revealed he rented an apartment near the Honolulu Zoo. When the couple mentioned they were from Cleveland, the young man abruptly excused himself to go to the bathroom and never returned to his seat. After the couple got home, they saw a news

Age progression photo of Ted Conrad. *U.S. Marshals Service, Cleveland Office.*

report about the Society National Bank theft and recognized the young man in the pictures as the same person they had encountered in the bar. The couple went to the authorities with their information. Apparently, a lot of the details the young man in the bar revealed about himself dovetailed with what was known about Ted Conrad.

Authorities followed every lead from Hawaii to Australia. They continued to monitor family and friends' phone calls. Mindful of Ted's hobbies of billiards and golf, the FBI placed ads in golfing and billiards magazines. They even contacted Steve McQueen. An FBI agent would attend Lakewood High School 1967 class reunions. As late as 2010, an agent visited Russell Metcalf. The only thing they've learned is that the trail has gone cold, and Ted had a lot of money to cover his tracks.

After fifty years, the case still haunts John Elliott. He has stayed informed on the hunt for Ted Conrad through his son U.S. marshal Pete Elliott, who heads up the Northern District of Ohio. The elder has said that the warrant (for Ted's arrest) is his. "One of the reasons I stayed after this guy is that some people thought he was some kind of hero or Robin Hood," he told both McKay and Jim Nicholas from the *Plain Dealer* in 2008. "He's not. He was nothing but a thief—a young, smart-assed thief who managed to elude law enforcement for all these years. Hopefully, we can bring him to justice soon."

Marshal Pete Elliott said, "Tips have come in over the years, and we take a look at them. We even had a tip that he was in England." None of the tips have panned out so far. "But we continue to work it."

In 2015, Marshal Elliott and the Northeast Regional Adult Parole director Todd Ishee expanded the Northern Ohio Violent Fugitive Task Force to include a Cold Case Unit. One of the first cold cases the task force looked at was Ted Conrad.

There has been a lot of speculation about where Ted is. Because he was fluent in French, Canada comes to mind, as do other French-speaking countries. Perhaps he saw the remake of *The Thomas Crown Affair* and knows that it was filmed on the French Caribbean island of Martinique.

"He could be anywhere," Marshal Pete Elliott commented. "He could be a lot of places."

On an Investigation Discovery channel show, *Lake Erie's Coldest Cases*, Renner brought up a possible sighting of Ted in Hawaii on an older episode of Anthony Bourdain's *No Reservations*. The man, who was a hermit and lived on a volcano, looked somewhat like an older version of Ted. The man was refusing to leave his home even though the volcano was threatening to erupt. Both Marshal Pete Elliott and Metcalf were certain the man was not Ted.

After all this time, one might wonder if Ted is still alive. The Elliotts think he is. "It's a gut feeling," the younger Elliott says. "I think he probably has grandchildren. He's probably lived a good life. He had all that money. He probably got married and has a family. He probably had a whole different identity and his family doesn't even know who he is. He's the only one who knows. He was smart and educated."

Renner thinks he's still alive. In spite of what Marshal Elliott and Russell Metcalf think, he still wonders if he could have been the man in an old episode of *No Reservations*. "He looked like the strange old man they found living on the top of a volcano in Hawaii."

When Metcalf is asked if his friend is still alive, he simply says, "I hope so."

3
LOOTING THE LIBRARY

David C. Breithaupt was a rare book thief with the perfect job. As the night circulation manager at the Olin and Chalmers Libraries on the Kenyon College campus in Gambier, Ohio, he oversaw general operations and student employees. His work hours of 5:00 p.m. to 2:00 a.m. with hardly anyone keeping track of him could not have been more conducive for his thievery. It gave him access to all the books he wanted.

At the time, the library was two conjoined buildings. A new library is due to open sometime in 2021. It is well known for its special collection of rare book treasures and manuscripts. The college publishes the *Kenyon Review*, a literary gem that printed the early works of such authors as Flannery O'Connor, Robert Penn Warren, Boris Pasternak, Dylan Thomas, Maya Angelou and Rita Dove. The magazine was founded in 1939 by John Crowe Ransom, its first editor.

Breithaupt was raised in Mount Vernon, Ohio, only five miles down the road from Kenyon. A graduate of Mount Vernon High School, he had dabbled in college classes at Columbus College of Art in Design while working at the Clintonville Public Library. According to Travis McDade in his book *Disappearing Ink*, Breithaupt also gained some book experience while living in New York, where he had worked a short time for the New York Public Library. His résumé also reflected jobs at New York bookstores and five years doing archive work for Allen Ginsberg, a respected Beat poet and a core member of the Beat Generation writers.

An aerial view of Kenyon College at Gambier, Ohio. *Kenyon College Library.*

Breithaupt was bewitched by books and probably could not believe his luck when he landed the job at Kenyon. He began stealing from the library's collection almost as soon as he was hired in October 1990. During the ten-year period before he was caught, he pilfered an estimated $50,000 worth of books, manuscripts and letters from the main collection, the Special Collections reading room and rare books stacks.

Librarians at Kenyon thought Breithaupt was peculiar and noticed his fixation with books. Book collectors would call his obsession bibliomania. Maybe he was too fond of books, but he got along with just about everyone. For one thing, he spent a lot of time in the Special Collections reading room and rare books stacks. No one realized that night after night, he was stealing books. Custodians sometimes saw him taking books to his car at quitting time, but they did not seem to think too much of it because he was a supervisor. They did not realize that he never brought the books back.

For the first five years, he had easy access to what he wanted because he was in possession of the key to the Special Collections reading room, as well as a library master key, which opened the door to the rare books room. Both

An aerial view of the Olin and Chalmers Libraries. *Kenyon College Library.*

rooms were on the lower level. At one point, the administration decided to tighten up the rules on keys. Breithaupt turned in his key to the reading room but quietly kept the library master that would give him access to the rare books.

The loss of the Special Collection key presented a problem for Breithaupt, so he had to invent ways to get into the room. Sometimes he struck it lucky. The best case was if someone forgot to lock the reading room door when they left for the day. But that hardly ever happened. The director's secretary had a key, so sometimes Breithaupt sat at her computer and hoped she had not locked her desk.

If neither of those things happened, he asked the custodians who cleaned the lower level to let him into the reading room. He had made friends with them and offered a variety of flimsy excuses for needing to get into the room. One of those excuses was that he had lost his key. (Apparently, they did not know he was not supposed to have a key.) Another was that his key was bent and did not work. Sometimes he just wandered into the room as the custodian was cleaning it. His favorite excuse was that he needed to use the

The Olin and Chalmers Libraries. *Kenyon College Library.*

magnifying glass. One of the custodians later said she never saw him use it, but she did see him use a key to go into the rare book room. She thought it was all right, though, because he worked there. After hearing the same excuses time after time, one of the custodians just handed Breithaupt the key when he asked to be let into the room.

When Breithaupt first started stealing books from the library, he hoarded them, stashing them in the one-story farmhouse on Caves Road east of Gambier where he lived with his girlfriend, Christa Hupp, and her two daughters. He and Hupp were always strapped. His $10,000 a year salary and Hupp's child support and job at the *Mount Vernon News* were not enough to cover their living expenses, her two daughters' college tuition, an aging furnace and flooded basement, plus other upkeep on their 1890 farmhouse.

Although Breithaupt had an obsession with books, he had never bothered to learn much about them or the book business. At first, he sold some of the books by going from book dealer to book dealer. He and Hupp called their business Caves Curve Books, because their house was located on a large curve. He and Hupp found dealers in book journals and sent out postcards with amateurish descriptions. Breithaupt sat on the computer at work at night and sent emails to friends and other possible buyers.

Hupp made all the business decisions and handled the money. As the internet grew, so did their business. When she found online Bibliofind and eBay in 1998 and 1999, respectively, their business began to skyrocket. Soon they were making more than $1,000 a month. At the top of their game, they were selling to people in nineteen states and four countries, but they were still broke much of the time.

Since the couple lacked experience, they made grievous mistakes in pricing, and their descriptions of books were amateurish. They sent out books that had pencil markings or water stains from where they had attempted to peel out Kenyon's book plates from the endpapers.

They sold an astronomy text that was made in 1528 for $4,750. Replacement value would have been $7,000. Other books made in the fifteenth and sixteenth centuries went up for sale and sold well below their value. At one point, Hupp listed 650 books for sale. Breithaupt gave his family books as presents. A first edition of *Huckleberry Finn* went to one of his brothers. It was worth more than $2,200.

One of their customers asked to pay with PayPal, but the couple declined. Breithaupt explained that they took only cash or checks. They did not want any electronic trails for tax purposes.

And then one night in the late 1990s, Breithaupt stumbled onto the archives in the filing cabinets in the Special Collections reading room. The drawers contained folders with handwritten letters, manuscripts and papers from hundreds of authors, including Thomas Pynchon, Joyce Carol Oates, Woody Allen and Flannery O'Connor, and none of these papers appeared to be catalogued.

He began by stealing single pieces. Emboldened, he snatched more and more until he stole whole files. It would be this act that led to his discovery.

On April 25, 2000, Bill Richards, a librarian at Georgia College and State University in Milledgeville, Georgia, was browsing on eBay when he came across the offer of a letter written by Flannery O'Connor. Milledgeville had been O'Connor's home from 1951 to 1964, when she died. The Georgia College and State University owned a large collection of her papers.

The letter on eBay, dated December 30, 1952, was addressed to John Crowe Ransom, the editor of the highly respected *Kenyon Review*. In one sentence, O'Connor asked him to return her short story "The River" and asked him to consider instead another story, "The Life You Save May Be Your Own." The *Review* eventually published five of her short stories, with "The Life You Save

Flannery O'Connor letter stolen from the library's special collection room started the investigation into David Breithaupt. It was later returned. *Kenyon College Library.*

May Be Your Own" being the first. That story and three others would go on to win O. Henry Awards. Richards knew this letter was extremely valuable, and he could hardly believe the eBay seller wanted only $500.

After Richards put in a bid, he realized something did not seem right, so he and an assistant did some research. In their own collection, they found a photocopy of the letter. The photocopy had a stamp on it that identified the original as belonging to the Kenyon College Library archives.

Richards canceled his online bid and reported the letter to eBay as being stolen. The report also went to Breithaupt. Richards then called Kenyon College's Christopher Barth, librarian and technology consultant, and told him what he had found. "Mr. Richards notified both Mr. Breithaupt and myself that he was suspicious of the letter," Barth, a Kenyon alumnus, wrote. He answered questions about Breithaupt and the theft through email.

Barth had not been in his position long and was looking for ways to make the collection more secure and tighten the rules on visiting Special Collections. Unknowingly, he even mentioned his ideas to Breithaupt. "David was soft-spoken and bookish," Barth remembered.

After getting off the phone with Richards, Barth checked the archive drawers and found O'Connor's complete file, as well as others, gone. He did not think a researcher took them; he figured the culprit had to be someone with keys.

Barth went to the vice president for library and info services, Dan Temple. They decided the first thing was to sort out the damage; then they could look for the culprit.

Breithaupt would make the latter easy for them.

Not long after Barth left Temple's office, Breithaupt appeared at Temple's door. Breithaupt had become friendly with Temple and often stopped by the administrator's office before his shift at the library to chat about favorite books or local history. Temple had a report from two days earlier that Breithaupt was asking to get into the Special Collections room after Barth had blocked it. Temple was going to address that with Breithaupt, but he did not get the chance.

Breithaupt, being the seller of the stolen O'Connor letter, had received a copy of the email from Richards, so his visit to Temple's office may have come from of a guilty conscience or, most likely, fear of being caught. Oddly, he started out by telling Temple that Hupp was having cancer surgery. He and Temple had never talked about their personal lives before, so this surprised Temple. After eliciting Temple's sympathy, Breithaupt went on to say that he had received the email about the stolen O'Connor letter. He admitted being in possession of the letter but said he had found it between the pages of a book he had bought at a sale. Temple was shocked but did not let on. He asked Breithaupt to bring the letter in to him. Breithaupt also emailed Barth explaining how he came to be in possession of the letter. He said he would drop the letter off.

"Mr. Breithaupt then returned the letter to the library with the explanation that he found it in a book at a book sale," Barth related.

Breithaupt wanted to return the letter, in spite of Hupp's resistance. She did not want to lose the $500 the letter would bring. Hupp, originally from South Bend, Indiana, was a pretty, dark-haired woman ten years Breithaupt's senior. It seemed as though she called the shots most of the time.

Barth and Temple were astonished by Breithaupt's admission. It was hard for them to believe he was capable of stealing from the library. They thought he did not even have keys.

For the next couple of days, Barth continued to gather evidence. He searched eBay and found transactions for books that sounded like they belonged to Kenyon. Then he went to see if those books were on the shelves where they belonged. Sure enough, they were missing.

Five days after the phone call from Bill Richards in Georgia, Barth and Temple suspended Breithaupt without pay and called in the authorities. The Knox County Sheriff's Office served a search warrant at the Caves Road farmhouse where Breithaupt and Hupp lived. They were greeted at the door by Breithaupt and his attorney William Kepko. Hupp was recovering from cancer surgery and not at home. Kepko advised his client to cooperate.

"His house was searched several times," Barth said. "Materials seized during that search were made evidence for the criminal case....The college arranged for two additional searches independently with Mr. Breithaupt through his attorney." At first, Breithaupt was not in favor of allowing this, but Kepko talked him into it.

The house was a cluttered mess, according to McDade's book. Shelves were loaded with books. Books were piled on tables, shoved in closets and stacked on chairs. They were heaped on the floor, on countertops and dressers. Any flat surface was covered with books. It was up to Barth and Temple to wade through the turmoil and determine which books belonged to Kenyon. "We identified items with ownership markings from Kenyon or other libraries, inventoried them, and then provided evidence of ownership for any materials we could prove were ours," Barth wrote. "Any materials for which we could not prove ownership were returned."

That first day, Barth and his colleagues were able to identify and reclaim 164 books and manuscripts. At the end of the second day, Barth along with director of safety and security Dan Werner and librarian Thomas House discovered 300 books that belonged to Kenyon and other Ohio colleges, most over one hundred years old. Just as they thought they were finished, Barth noticed a small outbuilding. Peeking through the window, he could see it was crammed full of books.

When they attempted to get into the building, Breithaupt blocked the way, saying it was not part of the agreement. He said the contents belonged to Hupp, and they needed her permission to enter. When they were able to go back, the books in the building had been sorted out and many were gone.

Hupp took over their legal decisions once she got home. The couple began to stonewall the investigation, and Kepko later resigned. Toward the end of May, the FBI was called in because the stolen items were sold for over $100,000 and across states lines.

During questioning, Breithaupt was under the influence of Xanax. FBI agents confronted him with a list of books they found on Hupp's computer. He told agents the books came from a book sale in Johnstown and from Kenyon's discards on the loading dock. He continued with these same lies throughout the investigation.

The investigation moved at a snail's pace, continuing into the summer of 2001. Kenyon officials were getting impatient. They wanted justice and were tired of waiting. Finally, in July 2001, the college filed a civil lawsuit against Breithaupt and Hupp, even though the school knew the couple had no money. The college's suit focused on getting its books back. It also asked for a restraining order to stop the sale of any more books.

Hupp decided the couple should countersue. They could not afford an attorney, so they filed the suit pro se (on behalf of themselves). As a defense to Kenyon's suit, they claimed the library had thrown the books away and Breithaupt rescued them from the trash. The couple asserted that the college was using them as scapegoats because they had brought to light the library's lack of care for valuable books. Their suit said that Barth and Werner had purposely intimidated them when the warrant was served at Caves Curve Farm, and this had caused them "humiliation and great emotional stress." Their suit further claimed that Barth and Werner took books that belonged to Hupp and Breithaupt and refused to return them. They asked for $10 million and a jury trial.

The legal wrangling dragged on from July 2001 to the trial in January 2003. The court docket for their case showed more than 110 entries. Hupp and Breithaupt were uncooperative during the preliminary proceedings, and they did not produce documents or show up for depositions. When Breithaupt did manage to show up, he was under the influence of either drugs or alcohol. He was unprepared and evasive, claiming he could not remember specifics. He mostly spun the same old confusing outright lies. The attorneys had heard them all before: Breithaupt dug valuable books out from a sack of paperbacks left on the library's dock for disposal; he bought them at the antiques mall; he bought them at a book sale. During one of the depositions, Hupp got up and left because she did not like some of the questions.

At one point, the pair hired James Burns, an attorney from a Cleveland firm. Where they got the money to hire him was unknown. By the time he was on the case, the couple had already made too many bad decisions.

On the morning of the trial, Judge Otho Eyster encouraged the parties to sit down and settle the matter. The college was in favor of settling. All the Kenyon representatives wanted was to get their books back, but Hupp and Breithaupt refused.

The trial lasted four days, during which the couple's financial records showed unexplained deposits from 1995 to 2000 of non-wage money of nearly $745,000. After listening to Breithaupt's lies and an implausible witness, who claimed to be with Breithaupt when he called librarians' attention to some of the rare books being deaccessioned and thrown out, the jury dismissed Breithaupt and Hupp's counterclaim. According to the *Columbus Dispatch*, the jury did not believe the books were found in the trash on the library's loading dock. They found the couple liable for "unjust enrichment and conversion," the civil equivalent of theft, and awarded Kenyon with $965,000 plus interest.

Hupp prepared an appeal to Ohio's Fifth District Court. She argued that Kenyon had "abused discovery preventing defendants' preparation for trial," and that the trial court had permitted irrelevant evidence (financial records, O'Connor's letter, eBay account and so on) that unduly influenced the jurors. The court rejected both arguments.

Hupp then got busy on an appeal to the Ohio Supreme Court. The couple was turned down there, too.

"The whole episode took a very long time," Barth said. By the time of the trial, he had become the director of information resources.

After four years, David C. Breithaupt was finally indicted and charged with illegally selling archaeological resources. In September 2004, he pleaded guilty. He was sentenced to twelve months in prison followed up by twelve months' probation. He was to pay $50,248 in restitution to Kenyon College for its costs of recovering the books he sold—on top of the nearly $1 million he owed from the civil suit. He also agreed to help locate the books and manuscripts that were sold. As part of his plea deal, federal prosecutors would drop additional charges and not charge Hupp.

Christa Hupp died in 2013.

Many of the rare books and treasured manuscripts Breithaupt stole have never been recovered.

4

WHO WAS COWBOY HILL?

Arthur "Cowboy" Hill used so many aliases, he might have forgotten his real name. He went by the names Joseph "Joe" Muzzio, W.B. Johnson, William X. Baker, "Gingerale" Jack and dozens of others.

He was probably born either Arthur Hill or Joseph Muzzio.

As Hill, he was part Native American with copper-colored skin, black hair and slate-colored eyes, according to Bertillon records from the Ohio State Penitentiary. But at times, he was described as a "negro" or "colored." His roots are not known. He could have been born down around the Texas-Mexican border to a Mexican father and Native American mother, as a 1921 article in the *Moline Dispatch* suggested. This might hold some truth, as he spoke some Spanish. Or he could have been born in Helena, Montana, in 1887, which is what is listed as his birthplace in the 1910 U.S. Census. At the time, he was incarcerated under the name Arthur Hill in the New York prison system at Auburn. "Montana 1887" is also listed as his birthplace in the 1930 census; he was in prison under the name W.B. Johnson in the Ohio State Penitentiary. But on both censuses, his race was listed as white.

Whether his real name was Arthur Hill or Joseph Muzzio, for certain he was a robber, safe cracker, burglar and dangerous criminal who knew no fear. At five feet, eight inches tall and 158 pounds, he was a master of escape, fast on his feet and quick to pull his two automatic pistols.

The earliest report of his criminal activities started in August 1904. A one-paragraph article in the *Plain Dealer* called him Keokawho and said he was a seventeen-year-old Kiowa from Montana. Another *Plain Dealer* article from 1913 reported he was born in Cleveland. This might have some weight to it because a Cleveland woman he had known since childhood posted bail for him during one of his scrapes. The 1920 census shows a Joseph Muzzio living on Murray Hill in Cleveland, and the age lines up. Wherever he came from, he was well known to authorities in several states. His story is filled with bold robberies, daring escapes and police shootouts.

Cowboy Hill started showing up on police watch lists and in newspaper articles in the early 1900s as the gang leader of car burglars in the Gordon Park neighborhood of Cleveland. He was a juvenile at that point in his criminal career. As time went on, he began to burgle houses and saloons, rob banks and jewelry stores and blow safes. Somewhere along the line he picked up the moniker "Cowboy."

Cleveland police dealt with him several times and regarded him as one of the most dangerous criminals to operate in their city. Officers were often told to shoot him on sight. Cowboy Hill's criminal history is long and as complicated as his nativity. Criminal types gravitated to him as a leader. Throughout his criminal career, he was associated with some of the most desperate crooks law enforcement would ever deal with.

In October 1909, he and two others threw a brick through the Augustus Firsch jewelry store window in Albany, New York, and made away with several thousand dollars in diamonds. Albany authorities put out a warrant on him. Days later, Patrolman Goodrich of Cleveland's fourth precinct spotted him on East Fifty-Fifth Street near St. Clair Avenue. Goodrich ordered Hill to halt, but the thief took off running. Goodrich pulled out his gun and began to fire. Hill was drawing away from Goodrich, attempting to scale a fence, when a bullet hit him in the back.

As he was recovering in St. Clair Hospital, one of his pals tried to spring him. The man waited until after midnight and then climbed through Hill's hospital window. He was carrying a revolver, some blankets and food. Police suspected Hill might make an attempt at escape, so Lieutenant Detective Alfred Walker and other detectives were waiting and foiled the effort.

After Hill recovered from his bullet wound, he was taken back to New York to answer for the jewelry store robbery. At the same time, Cleveland police wanted him for a 1907 burglary, but that case was nolled (dismissed) in deference to the more serious New York charge. The state reformatory at Mansfield was also after him for parole violation, but the jewelry store robbery took precedence. Hill served eighteen months for taking the jewels. Mansfield authorities were waiting at the gate when Hill was released from Auburn, but he slipped through their hands and headed back to Cleveland.

Mug shot of "Cowboy" Hill, a.k.a. W.B. Johnson, a.k.a. Joseph Muzzio. *Ohio History Connection.*

At the time, Cleveland police believed him to be one of the men who had robbed several saloonkeepers in the city. On Saturday night, June 8, 1912, Hill was crossing Public Square when Detective Moore caught sight of him. Gun in hand, Moore gave chase. Hill, being faster than his pursuer, dodged the bullets and tore down an alley off East Sixth Street and headed toward Rockwell Avenue.

Patrolman Hall, who was on St. Clair NE at the time, heard the gunshots and headed in that direction. By coincidence, he chose the same alley as Cowboy Hill. The two met in the middle behind the White garage. Hill started to draw his gun. The cop grabbed Hill's gun hand, and at the same time, attempted to pull his own weapon. Hill seized the lawman's gun hand.

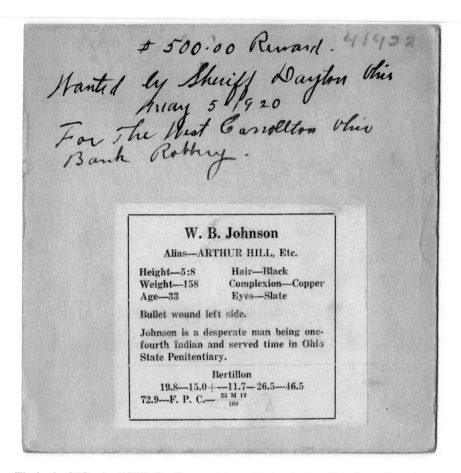

$ 500.00 Reward. 4/4/22
Wanted by Sheriff Dayton Ohio
May 5 1920
For The West Carrollton Ohio
Bank Robbery.

W. B. Johnson

Alias—ARTHUR HILL, Etc.

Height—5:8   Hair—Black
Weight—158   Complexion—Copper
Age—33   Eyes—Slate

Bullet wound left side.

Johnson is a desperate man being one-fourth Indian and served time in Ohio State Penitentiary.

Bertillon
19.8—15.0+—11.7—26.5—46.5
72.9—F. P. C.— $\frac{25 \text{ M } 19}{100}$

The back of "Cowboy" Hill's Bertillon card shows his description. *Ohio History Connection.*

The two were locked in a desperate struggle. A crowd gathered, but no one tried to help Patrolman Hall—probably for fear of being shot. At last, a woman stepped up and bravely snatched Hall's keys from his pocket and ran to the closest police (Murphy) call box.

An automobile drove into the alleyway and stopped outside the garage door. One of its occupants got out to assist the officer. Hill let go of Hall and drew back to punch the motorist. That gave Hall the opportunity to go for his nightstick and strike a blow.

Cowboy Hill was arraigned the next morning and held on $300 bond. He secured the bail money from Jean Arneda, who lived at Perkins Avenue NE. She said he was a childhood friend, and he had talked her into handing over

Police call box. *Author's collection.*

her life savings to his lawyer for bail. Two days later, Hill jumped bail and left the young woman with nothing more than a crumpled-up note. The *Plain Dealer* ran the wording of the note in the June 16 paper: "Hello Kiddo: this can't last forever. This is my attorney. Give him $300 and he will see that I get out on bail; I will come back for trial. Arthur"

The young woman said Abram E. Bernsteen, Hill's attorney, delivered the note to her house. She then accompanied Bernsteen to his office, where she forked over the money.

"I didn't think Arthur would do that; he told me he would appear on the day set for his trial," she told the reporter. "I have known Arthur all my life; we used to go to school together, and when he was in trouble I wanted to help him."

Over the next few days, Cleveland police hunted Hill in several places over the city, including the waterfront, but he was always a step ahead. Finally, Detectives Snyder, Koehlke, Shipley and Breen got wind that their prey was holed up in a rooming house on Oregon Avenue. Sunday morning, August 25, they went after him. The next day's issue of the *Cleveland Leader* reported the capture.

Koehlke took up a position at the back of the house. Snyder stayed outside on the sidewalk, and Shipley and Breen knocked on the door. The landlord, Max Levy, answered and directed the detectives to Hill's room at the front of the house. The cops instructed him to knock on Hill's door and say he had a telegram for him. Levy did as he was told, but Hill did not open the door.

Shipley and Breen forced the door open. The room was empty, but the window was open. Snyder, out on the sidewalk, saw Hill climb out the window onto the front porch roof. Snyder drew his revolver and aimed it at Hill. "Throw up your hands!"

Taken by surprise, Hill complied.

"No monkey business or your head goes off," Snyder barked. He then ordered Hill to slide down the porch post to the ground. Hill did as he was told. When Hill's feet touched ground, Snyder shoved his gun in his face.

"You needn't act like such a roughneck," Hill said as he was handcuffed.

Left: Abram E. Bernsteen was Cowboy Hill's Cleveland attorney. *Cleveland Public Library.*

Below: Abram E. Bernsteen (*right*), Hill's attorney, and Howell Leuck were U.S. attorneys. *Cleveland Public Library.*

Cowboy Hill was found guilty of burglary, larceny and jumping bail. He was sent back to the state reformatory in Mansfield. Days after he was installed there, a sheriff from Illinois came calling. It seems that Hill was wanted at Crown Point, Illinois, as the leader of a gang that floated worthless checks up into the thousands. Later that year, authorities decided Hill was too vicious to be jailed at Mansfield, so they transferred him to the Ohio State Penitentiary to serve out his eight-year sentence. Somehow, he entered the prison under the alias of W.B. Johnson.

On August 28, 1913, Hill/Johnson walked away from the prison. He had conned prison guards into thinking he was a man with the same name who was a trusty due to be released the next day. Unknowingly, the prison attendants sent him to a low-security area to repair the porch on the prison stables. Officials thought another escapee picked him up in an automobile.

On the loose, Hill was up to his old tricks. He blew post office safes in Seneca and Cadmus, Michigan, and a safe in Seneca, Ohio. Adrian police believed he participated in a Grand Rapids jewelry store robbery where two clerks were shot to death. They also thought he was responsible for several robberies around the Toledo area.

In late October 1913, a Wabash freight train crew grew suspicious of Hill because he was hanging around the rail yards in Adrian. Police in that city chased him for five miles over open country. The *Ann Arbor News* reported that he laughed at the "volleys of shots that followed him." According to the paper, Hill was finally captured when he ran out of breath. He had two revolvers on him as well as an electric explosive device, which cops believed was his own invention. He gave "Gingerale" Jack Johnson as his name. A week later, they found out his real name.

While he was incarcerated in the Lenawee County Jail, he wrote several love letters to a Mrs. Louis Muzzio, who he said was his wife. The *Daily Telegram*, an Adrian newspaper, reported the letters revealed expert penmanship, perfect spelling, proficient vocabulary and well-turned phrases. There were occasional expressions in Spanish. The letter also revealed that he possessed considerable financial resources. If the letter was to be believed, Cowboy Hill held railroad stock worth $1,200 and $8,000 cash in a Toledo bank.

While in the Lenawee jail, he could not resist the temptation to escape. Guards found broken bars on his cell before he was able to make his getaway.

Lenawee County undersheriff Fred Nutten and his deputy took a shackled Hill back to the Ohio State Penitentiary, where they were greeted by four to five hundred lawmen from all around Ohio, according to the

Daily Telegram. It seems the crowd of detectives and police wanted to lay eyes on the scoundrel.

On the trip back to the penitentiary, Hill chatted quite a bit with his captors about his many escapades. He made a prediction that he would be back with his pals again "when the birds begin to sing."

For whatever reason, Hill did not serve out his full twelve-year sentence. By 1920, he was back on the streets with his pals and "the birds began to sing."

Cowboy Hill and three other men walked into the West Carrollton bank in Montgomery County on Saturday morning, April 10, 1920, and drew their guns. They didn't bother to wear masks or care how many people in the street outside saw them.

Two of them walked up to cashier W.E. Dean and assistant cashier Alice M. Rietdyk, pointed their revolvers at them and demanded the cash on hand. The bandits bound Alice's hands and forced her into the vault, then instructed Dean to fork over the dough. Dean surrendered the $15,000 payroll money earmarked for West Carrollton Parchment Company and the American Envelope Company. Another $7,200 from the day before was also taken.

Just then Edward Beckett walked into the bank to cash a check and found himself looking down the barrel of a gun. He was told to face the wall. He complied.

Charles Christian, a salesman from the parchment company, was the next customer through the doors. He, too, was met with the business end of a revolver. The thugs ordered him to put up his hands and face the wall. He resisted and was pistol-whipped.

By this time, one of the robbers had escorted Dean into the safety deposit vault, where the thug grabbed between $4,000 and $5,000 in Liberty bonds, as well as other securities.

Fourteen-year-old Chester Holliday and a woman named Elizabeth Kohler had the bad luck to enter the bank at this point. One of the robbers hit the boy in the back of the head and ordered the two into the vault.

Dean, Rietdyk and the bank customers were herded to the back of the vault. The *Dayton Daily News* reported there was a six-year-old among the victims. The news story stated there were seven victims in all. One was relieved of $250, and the child lost his penny.

The robbers left the bank and jumped into what was described as a waiting blue Hudson touring car with red wheels. Before taking off, one of them flipped the license plate up so it could not be read. They motored toward Dayton at top speed.

West Carrollton's Marshal Waldo Recher deputized three men, and they took off in pursuit of a Buick touring car. They chased the robbers down the Cincinnati Pike until the bandits reached Springboro Pike and turned south.

Back at the bank, Alice Rietdyk told Deputies Hiram Slattery and Howard Webster one of the culprits had been in the bank three times that morning before the robbery. She said he was a short, heavy-set man, well-dressed in a blue overcoat and slouch hat. The first time he came into the bank, he was looking for a city directory. She told him the bank did not have a city directory, so she gave him a telephone book. He left. A half hour later, he was back. This time he wanted a traction car schedule. She gave him the times. He left again. He returned a third time wanting to know about the rate of pay at the parchment company. Rietdyk thought he was looking for a job, so she gave him as much information as she knew.

The fourth time the stranger entered the bank, he was accompanied by three other men—all brandishing guns. Rietdyk described two of his companions as white, shabbily dressed and small, maybe weighing 125–30 pounds. She described the fourth man as a tall "colored man" wearing overalls.

Alice Rietdyk said one of them pointed his gun at her and told her to keep quiet "unless she wanted to die." Another one of the robbers went into the bank's safe, where Dean was working. The bandit leveled his weapon at Dean and threatened to shoot him unless Dean did what he was told. The third and fourth men stood guard in the lobby, probably to take care of customers who entered the bank. Dean said he thought there was a fifth man waiting in the car.

The robbers got away with somewhere north of $22,000 in cash plus the Liberty bonds. Bank officials assured the public that their money was protected by burglary insurance. The Dayton bank sent money to the Carrollton bank to cover the parchment and envelope companies' payrolls.

The Peoples Savings Bank of Delta (Ohio) was the next stop for Cowboy Hill and his pals. This time they were driving a large seven-passenger greenish-blue Cadillac, according to the *Delta Atlas*. They pulled up in front of the bank on May 20, 1920, at 10:20 a.m. Leaving the motor running and one man behind the wheel, Hill and six of his cronies entered the bank.

Assistant cashier M.W. Casler was in the cashier's cage waiting on Davis Dodge when a stranger approached the window and pushed the customer away. Pulling a gun, the man growled, "Give me a blank receipt."

All of a sudden three men leaped over the railing at the cashier's desk. One seized Casler. Another grabbed Jesse Bloomer, the bookkeeper. A third reached for Candace Haley, the second assistant cashier, but before he could lay a hand on her, she set off the burglar alarm. "You started that alarm, now you stop it," one of the thugs ordered. She refused.

Both women and Dodge were herded into the back room and made to stand against the wall. One of the crooks held them against the back wall throughout the whole ordeal. "Close your eyes, and do as we tell you. We don't want to hurt anyone."

One of the bandits guarded the front door to get the drop on unlucky customers who entered the bank. Out in the street, James F. Flavelle, Roy Champlain and Arthur Beckler heard the ringing alarm and went inside. They were greeted by a man with a large gun and ushered into the back room with the others.

According to the paper, another member held a "big rapid fire gun" on Casler and made him turn off the alarm. The thug then forced Casler to open the strong vault where the money was kept. Once the money was scooped into a bag the gangsters had brought with them, Casler was ordered into the room where the others were being held. One of the robbers struck Casler over the head with the butt of his gun as the cashier walked past him. "There, damn you. Take that."

By that time, several people had gathered outside the bank. The robbers burst out of the doors and wildly fired their guns, spraying the street with bullets as they made their way to the car. At least thirty to fifty rounds whizzed through the air. One bullet passed seventy feet through the Wagoner Bakery and struck James Warner at the back of the store. A.M. Wilkins was luckier. A bullet went through his coat pocket, tore a piece of paper and broke his pipe but did not harm him. Lead shattered the front plate-glass window of the Hotel Lincoln storeroom. Another round grazed Carl Sagert on the neck.

The robbers dove into the car and headed at high speed out of town east on Main Street toward Toledo. They got away with $12,000 in cash and $6,000 in Liberty bonds. Toledo police were notified immediately, and a ring of officers patrolled the entrances to the city. By 1:00 p.m., Toledo police had spotted the suspect car entering the city at Upton Avenue. They gave chase, but the Cadillac was too "high powered" for police vehicles to keep up.

The only real lead police had as to who the suspects were came from William Mohr of Fulton Township. He told police he was driving into Delta that morning, and at the Sheffield crossing he saw an automobile stop and pick up four men at Brigham's farm. A bit down the road, he saw the automobile stop again and pick up a man who was walking east.

American Casual Company offered a reward of "$1000 each for the apprehension and conviction of persons responsible for and implicated in the hold-up of the Peoples Saving Bank." The insurance company also offered $500 to any person who had information leading to the apprehension, arrest and conviction of the robbers.

Bank and insurance officials were sure the bank jobs in Delta and West Carrollton were pulled by the same gang. The reward grew to $5,000, according to an article in the *Dayton Herald*. Wanted posters with pictures of W.B. Johnson, a.k.a. Cowboy Hill, a.k.a. the Indian, a.k.a. the Chief; Archie James Knerr, alias Dennison; and two others were sent out. The suspects were indicted by a grand jury and warrants were issued.

Five days after the Delta robbery, Toledo police collared Edward T. O'Neil, a.k.a. Malady, who was one of Hill's gang. The bank's Jesse Bloomer and Candace Haley went to Toledo to view a lineup of ten men. O'Neil was the fifth man in the line. The *Delta Atlas* reported that Jesse Bloomer pointed at him. "That is the man, the one that held us up in the back corridor."

According to the news article, O'Neil said something to the effect of "Be careful, lady, I don't know what crime you are accusing me of, I have never been guilty of any crime in which you were interested and you should be careful what you say in charging a man." O'Neil was tried, convicted and sentenced to the Ohio State Penitentiary.

More money was added to the reward after Hill and his gang robbed the Commercial Bank in Moline, Illinois. This stickup was pulled with the same methods as the West Carrollton and Delta banks. Five men sprang into action, guns blazing, startling the cashiers and customers. They quickly relieved the bank and customers of $20,000.

As the robbers hit the street and headed for the Cadillac, they began firing their guns. The owner of the barbershop across the street was severely wounded when he opened his door to see what the ruckus was.

The desperadoes piled into their car, but it wouldn't start. One of the bandits dashed across the street and frantically attempted to steal a parked car, an expensive Moon Motor. Confronted by the owner, the thief fired a few shots. By this time, luck had returned to the thieves and the Cadillac started.

On Tuesday, September 14, 1920, Toledo police detectives decided to act on information they had been gathering over several months. They banged on the door of an apartment at 2220 Franklin Avenue in the city's fashionable West End neighborhood. They were looking for the men who had pulled various Ohio and Michigan bank and payroll robberies, including jobs in Lockland (Hamilton County), West Carrollton and Delta, Ohio. Chief of detectives William D. Delehanty said the raid was the culmination of investigations into multiple crimes over several months and searches of fifteen possible hideouts.

At least fourteen heavily armed lawmen climbed into five automobiles and headed for the Franklin Avenue address. They parked out of sight and quietly proceeded to the apartment. Ten of them, carrying riot guns and regular shotguns, surrounded the building with orders to guard the doors and windows. Four detectives took on the most dangerous position of going through the door.

At 9:30 a.m., Detective Stephen Quinn, Captain James M. O'Reilly and Detectives William C. Culver and August "Augie" Salhoff pounded on the door. Gang member Joe Forrest greeted them. Tall and bone thin, the forty-one-year-old Forrest was unarmed. He threw up his hands and offered no resistance when O'Reilly arrested him. Detectives warned him to be quiet while they checked the rest of the house.

Culver continued deeper into the apartment, his shotgun ready. He made his way down a hall to the dining room, where he saw a table set for five for breakfast. Thirty-two-year-old Archie Dennison confronted Culver at a bedroom doorway just off the hall. Clad in purple pajamas, a coat and brown oxfords with no socks, he had a bandage wrapped around his head. Culver demanded he give up.

"Never!" the bandit shouted and yanked a large semiautomatic pistol from his pocket. Culver was faster. Raising his shotgun hip-high, he fired one barrel just as Dennison bolted around the corner to the front room. The buckshot riddled the door full of holes and hit Dennison in the face.

Fatally wounded, the crook staggered into the next room, where O'Reilly was holding Forrest at gunpoint. There are various versions as to what happened next—probably because everything unfolded so fast. According to a *Plain Dealer* account, Quinn raced into the room and began struggling with Dennison. During the scuffle, the two lost their footing and crashed over a chair. A reporter for the *Toledo Blade* wrote that Dennison had been blinded when he was shot, and he stumbled into Quinn, who had his back to Dennison. One thing was for certain: Dennison pulled the trigger during the fray—whether by accident or on purpose—and the bullet struck Quinn in the right hip. A third version from an undated typed manuscript by an unknown author held in the Toledo Police Museum files claims that when Quinn and Dennison went down, it was Cowboy Hill who shot Quinn. Dennison rolled on top of Quinn, ready to pull the trigger a second time.

Above, left: Toledo police detective Stephen Quinn was wounded during the raid on the Toledo hideout. *Toledo Police Museum.*

Above, right: Toledo police captain James O'Reilly arrested Joe Forrest at the door of the Toledo hideout. *Toledo Police Museum.*

Left: Toledo police detective William Culver shot Archie Dennison at the Toledo hideout. *Toledo Police Museum.*

A separate story related to a retired Toledo police officer confirms that one of the other detectives shot Dennison point-blank, killing him instantly.

Meanwhile, waving his two .45 automatic pistols, Cowboy Hill, escaped out the rear door. Detective Robert F. Bartley and others were guarding the back of the building. They met him with a barrage of bullets from shotguns, pistols and a riot gun. Hill kept his fingers locked on the triggers of both his guns, shooting wildly into the yard until his weapons were nearly empty. Bartley remembered bullets buzzing past him. Knowing his life depended on it, he kept shooting his own gun. Hill's escape attempt was futile. Police kept firing on him until he dropped at the gate, wounded twenty-eight times.

A *Plain Dealer* account said he rolled over, fired the last round from his gun and yelled, "Take that!" The typed, undated report claimed Hill cried out, "Don't shoot anymore. You got me real good and proper."

More than one hundred shots had been fired. When the smoke cleared, two young women emerged from one of the bedrooms. One had been hiding under a bed, while the other had sought cover in a cedar chest. Billie Calhoun, twenty-five, was Dennison's girlfriend. Viola Cochran's age has been given as fifteen, twenty and twenty-four. She claimed to be the cook. In truth, she had a long criminal history. Neither woman seemed the least upset over the carnage. The detectives ordered the two to prepare to go to the police station. Both dressed in what was described in the papers as "handsome walking suits" and took the time to powder their noses. On the way out of the house, they stepped over Dennison's body, being careful not to get blood on their shoes. One of the women stopped and gave the dead man a cold last look and then continued outside to where the neighbors had collected. Calhoun and Cochran were taken to the detective bureau for questioning and then transferred to the Lagrange Street station.

Quinn and Hill were taken to Mercy Hospital. Quinn's wound was serious, but he would recover and return to duty. Hill's recovery would be a long road.

The bandage on Dennison's head covered a gunshot wound suffered two weeks earlier in the early morning hours of September 3 during a shootout with motorcycle officer Walter Kruse. Dennison's wound would have been fatal within a short time.

Kruse was seriously wounded during that encounter. He survived but was placed on disability. His brother, Louis Kruse, participated in the Franklin Avenue raid.

Joe Forrest cooperated with detectives. He had a receipt to a Dorr Street garage, where the cops found a car with numerous bullet holes. It fit the description of the touring car involved in the Kruse shooting on Vance Street near South Fifteenth.

Detectives combed the Franklin Avenue apartment for guns and money. They found high-powered rifles, numerous handguns, burglar tools and a large can of nitroglycerine and fuses for blowing safes. Curiously, the furnishings in the apartment were tasteful. Current magazines and books on philosophy were lying about, and artwork hung on the walls.

In addition, police found an eighteen-inch-high hammered silver cup with the inscription *Gar Wood-Chris Smith Trophy. Ten-mile handicap, Algonac, Labor Day, Sept. 5, 1920. Winner* ———. The name of the winner had not been inscribed. At first, police thought the cup was stolen, but further investigation revealed just how versatile the thieving gang was.

Two months after they robbed the People's Savings Bank at Delta, Hill, Dennison, Calhoun and Forrest adopted new names and assumed different roles in the summer resort Algonac, Michigan, where they passed themselves off as either oilmen or bond salesmen, depending upon the source. Hill took the name Joseph Morreau, Forrest adopted the last name of Kelley, Dennison became Arthur Densmore and Billie Calhoun Mrs. Densmore. To complete their new identities, they dressed smartly, conversed with polished speech and adopted impeccable manners.

They made friends easily and often hosted parties at their cottage. The men were graceful dancers. Kelley (or Forrest) was said to have been particularly witty. They had money to burn and several cars at their disposal.

The gang took frequent "business" trips. Their absences never caused suspicion among their new friends. It was assumed they were visiting their business headquarters or their safety deposit box. When they returned from these trips, their pockets were flush and deep. Later it was discovered their business was bank robbery.

They bought a powerboat for $6,000 from a Heart Beach boat builder named J.P. Perry. It was fast, but not fast enough to enter the regatta. They paid Chris Smith $4,500 for a new, more powerful engine and gave him an additional $300 to install it. The expense paid off because they won the 1920 Labor Day ten-mile handicap race.

Cowboy Hill spent the rest of 1920 on a stretcher in the Lucas County Jail. In January 1921, he pleaded guilty to possession of burglary tools. The court waived two more serious charges that carried heavier penalties. Hill was sentenced to prison for one to five years. His attorney told the judge Hill would receive better medical treatment at the Ohio State Penitentiary. Hill arrived at the penitentiary gates leaning on the shoulders of two other men.

He was released from the penitentiary in 1928, but the law was not finished with him. The sheriff of Fulton County was waiting at the prison gates to arrest him for the People's Savings Bank job. He was tried and convicted of that robbery and sentenced to fifteen more years.

When 322 prisoners were burned alive in their locked cells in a devastating fire at the Ohio State Penitentiary on April 21, 1930, Hill and others organized a mutiny that took several days to put down. The instigators spent time in isolation for their part. In 1934, Hill was turned down for parole.

Arthur "Cowboy" Hill led such a long and violent criminal career that it is hard to keep track of all his misdeeds. According to David Bailey, a researcher for the Toledo Police Museum, Hill is associated with a list of at least thirty other crooks, some of them murderers. They seemed to drift in and out of one another's gangs.

Hill was married to Emma Frances Howell Irons, a widow and little sister of a gang member. Emma got into trouble for being in possession of burglary tools. She had two daughters by her first marriage and one daughter by Hill. They married in Chatham-Kent, Ontario, Canada, according to a family genealogy, but a newspaper article reported that they entered into a common-law marriage. They filed a contract for marriage in Toledo on January 19, 1919. The name he gave for their marriage certificate was Joseph Muzzio. Emma called herself Mrs. J.T. Muzzio, and their daughter carried the last name of Muzzio.

Formal documents for Hill are mostly limited to arrest and penitentiary records. He was a robber, yegg (safe cracker), jewel thief and burglar. Sources also pointed to bootlegging and probably more. He was one of the first big-time bank robbers to use the automobile as a method of escape.

Released on parole on "imminent danger of death" in July 1937, Hill was taken to the Lucas County Hospital in Toledo. Newspapers reported Joseph Muzzio, also as known as "Cowboy" Hill, died of cancer on October 17, 1937.

Joseph Muzzio appears as his name on his death certificate, and Helena, Montana, is recorded as his place of birth. The Montana State Historical Society found no birth, school or church record of him.

5

CAUGHT ON CAMERA

T he trio had known one another for only a month before they robbed the St. Clair Savings & Loan Company at 6235 St. Clair Avenue NE in Cleveland on Friday, April 12, 1957. Little did they know it was the first bank heist to be captured on camera in the world.

A Photoguard camera system had been installed in the bank one day before the robbery. The surveillance camera was a collaboration of the Photoguard Corporation of New York and members of the Cleveland Division of Police. Thomas E. Story, the police department's superintendent of communications, came up with the idea of a surveillance camera. He worked with the police department's radio engineer, Bob Hover; electronic specialist Edward Kisiel; and photo technicians Ladis Lisy and John B. Kastner to adapt an army surplus gun camera. Al Jenkins of the New York company worked out any bugs and enclosed the camera in a watertight, dust-proof case. It captured the holdup in a two-minute film clip.

The financial institution had been robbed twice before. In 1955, robbers held up the bank and got away with $67,75. The bank lost $30,000 in a holdup in 1956. Police tracked down and caught that culprit.

As Steven Ray Thomas, Wanda DiCenzi and Rose Therese O'Donnell made their plans, they had no idea their faces would be splashed across television screens all over the country.

Twenty-four-year-old Thomas and his eighteen-year-old partners first met at the Forest Hill Restaurant near 138th Street and St. Clair Avenue NE. Thomas was down on his luck. He was broke and living in a rooming house.

The St. Clair Savings and Loan was the first bank to have a surveillance camera installed. *Cleveland Police Museum.*

He suffered from epilepsy and either could not find or keep a job because of it. His past included a brief record for discharging a firearm at a pizza place. He had also been questioned as a suspicious person in a separate incident.

Wanda DiCenzi's father said it was hard for him to believe that his daughter had anything to do with the robbery. "My daughter is a good girl," August DiCenzi told a *Plain Dealer* reporter. Wanda, who was blond but had tinted her hair red, left Collinwood High School after only two years. "But she was always a good student," her father said, adding that she participated in the music program and sang in the church choir. He told the reporter he had never seen Thomas. "Wanda is only 18, and never dated boys older than she."

About six weeks before the robbery, Wanda moved out because her father became upset when she stayed out late on Saturday nights. She went to stay with her friend, pretty, dark-haired Rose O'Donnell.

Cleveland police superintendent of communications Thomas E. Story. *Cleveland Police Museum.*

Although Rose had several siblings, she lived alone with her father on Blenheim Road NE in Cleveland and worked part time. Most importantly, she had a twenty-four-year-old boyfriend named Patsy Delligatta, and he had a car. Neighbors said the 1955 black and white Buick was in front of her home frequently.

On Thursday, April 11, Thomas approached the girls about the bank job while they were hanging out at the Forest Hill Restaurant. Wanda said, "Thomas came in and asked us to help him get some money from a bank."

"Let's rob a bank," he said.

The girls thought he was joking.

But the next morning, Rose drove Delligatta to work, and then she and Wanda drove his car down St. Clair Avenue NE to have a look at the bank. After casing it, they stopped to have lunch with a Pepsi Cola truck driver friend at Sern's Restaurant, 6036 St. Clair Avenue, a block west of the bank. Two Cleveland detectives, Joseph David and William Steele, were also eating lunch there. They happened to notice the attractive redhead and commented on the way she walked.

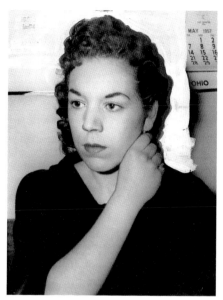 

Left: Wanda DiCenzi was one of the robbers of the St. Clair Savings and Loan. *Cleveland Public Library.*

Right: Steven Ray Thomas, one of the robbers caught on the first bank surveillance camera. *Cleveland Public Library.*

After lunch, Wanda and Rose drove to Thomas's rooming house on Saranac Road. When they got to his room, they found he was sick, so they left and drove around for a while. By the time they returned to Thomas's rooming house, he was ready to go.

Thomas directed Wanda to drive to an alley near the bank. Up until Rose parked the car, the girls still thought he was kidding. One of the girls quoted him as saying, "You've come this far. You can't back out now."

Right before 12:30 p.m., Thomas and Wanda got out of the car and headed into the bank, leaving Rose behind the wheel of the Buick with the motor running. Thomas tied a handkerchief over his mouth and nose, and Wanda covered her red-tinted hair with a scarf. He shoved Wanda through the door, pulled out a gun and announced his intentions to the tellers. The patrons were frightened, and some of them fled out the door. One of the cashiers had the wherewithal to press the button that started both the new camera rolling and turned on the police alarm.

While Thomas held the employees at gunpoint, Wanda went around the counter and stuffed $2,376 into a bag. The duo had no idea that a security camera was recording their whole illegal transaction.

Once all the money was stashed in the bag, Thomas and Wanda ran out of the bank and jumped into the Buick. Rose put the gas pedal down. They sped north on East 63rd Street, took a shortcut across a parking lot to East 64th Street and wound their way south to Superior. Near 118th Street they began to zigzag northeast until finally reaching Thomas's rooming house. There, they divvied up the money. It came to a bit more than $700 each.

Thomas grabbed his things, and the three piled back into Delligatta's Buick. They drove to East 147th Street, where the girls waited while Thomas rented a room in a different house. The next stop was at a cleaner, where the girls left him.

Flush with money, Wanda and Rose went shopping downtown. Rose parked Delligatta's car on Prospect Avenue. When they returned to the Buick from their shopping spree, they found a ticket for illegal parking on the windshield.

Two and a half hours after the holdup, police had distributed the two-minute robbery film from the Photoguard camera to the newspapers and television stations. The media wasted no time in getting the footage out to the public. Next, police sent copies of the film to the FBI in Washington, as well as to police departments in surrounding states.

Cleveland detectives viewed the film at afternoon roll call. Detectives David and Steele thought they recognized the girl as the same redhead they had seen at Sern's Restaurant while they were having lunch. It was her walk that caught their attention. They remembered she was eating with a truck driver.

Detectives Thomas Coughlin and Lesley Caldwell set out to find anyone who knew the girls at Sern's Restaurant. One of the waitresses at Sern's knew where the trucker worked and gave the information to the detectives. With that knowledge, Coughlin and Caldwell soon came up with a name by tracing him through the company that owned the truck. They paid a visit to the trucker, who admitted having a cup of coffee with a girl named Wanda, but he did not know her last name. He did know that she worked at a pizza place on Lorain Avenue. A worker at the pizza shop supplied Wanda's last name and said she worked as an usher at the Palace Theater.

The theater's supervisor told police that Wanda had quit on March 2 and that her mother was also searching for her. Late Friday evening, police visited Mrs. DiCenzi but didn't mention the robbery. She gave them photos of her daughter.

At this time, Wanda and Rose were completely unaware of the investigation. They were busy looking for a new place for Wanda to live.

Using part of the robbery money, they rented a place on Franklin Boulevard. After that, they returned the car to Delligatta and gave him $100. Later that night, they hitchhiked to Willoughby, where they spent the night in a hotel. In the morning, they hitchhiked back to Cleveland, still unaware of what was ahead.

Cleveland police detective Thomas M. Coughlin helped to identify the St. Clair Savings and Loan robbers. *Cleveland Public Library.*

Thomas had been watching television that evening. When he saw the newscast of the robbery, he panicked. "I almost fell on my face when I saw the pictures late Friday in the Cleveland news," he told a reporter. "All I wanted to do then was run." He caught the first bus out of Cleveland to Columbus, and from there, he went to Indianapolis. Every time he got near a phone, he called a friend in Cleveland who knew about the robbery and had seen the news. After each call, the friend reported to the police.

Rose O'Donnell was the first to give herself up. She told the *Plain Dealer*, "I didn't know what to think. I talked to my boyfriend [Delligatta], and we decided I should give myself up." At 7:30 p.m., a friend dropped her off at the FBI office in the Engineers Building. Agents turned her over to the police. She gave them her statement but denied receiving any money from the robbery.

Detectives searched Rose's room and found the parking ticket. The license number on the ticket led them to Patsy Delligatta. Delligatta was taken into custody. He told police Rose had borrowed his car on the day of the robbery.

When Thomas got to Indianapolis, a stranger started talking to him about the film. "He said he saw it in a bar up the street," Thomas told a *Plain Dealer* reporter. "That was too much for me. I knew I might as well turn around and give myself up."

Thomas took a bus back to Cleveland, and at 11:50 p.m. he walked into Central Police Headquarters. "I hear you're looking for me. I'm Thomas," he told the three patrolmen who were at the station.

Detectives questioned Thomas until long after midnight. While he was at the station, Detective John Oller, known for his "jolly appearance," came to the station. Oller was not involved in the case, but he was curious to set

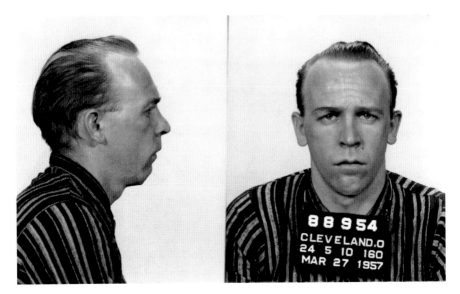

Mug shot of Steven Ray Thomas. *Cleveland Public Library.*

eyes on the robber. By happenstance, he crossed paths with Thomas and the other detectives in the hall. Thomas saw Oller's pleasant expression, and thinking the detective was making fun of him, the robber broke loose and slugged Oller in the eye. Thomas later apologized.

Interviewed by the *Plain Dealer*'s chief police reporter Robert E. Tidyman, Thomas said he had thrown away the .32-caliber Beretta he used in the holdup, adding that it shot only blanks. Police recovered the gun a few days later. It was a harmless automatic starter pistol that belonged to Delligatta's brother.

Minutes after Thomas turned himself in, an anonymous woman called police with information that a girl who looked "an awful lot like Wanda DiCenzi" was living at a rooming house at West Thirty-First Street and Franklin Boulevard NW. Within a half hour after the call, police had Wanda in custody. "I heard about the pictures on the radio," she said. "I didn't believe it."

By Sunday morning—just thirty-six hours after the robbery—the suspects were all in custody. Police recovered all but about $600 of the $2,376 the trio had stolen. Thomas spent some money on clothes and bus fare. He surrendered $597. At first, the girls would not admit to sharing any of the loot, but after a while, they confessed to spending at least $125 each on clothing. They paid rent and for a hotel room. Wanda returned $700. Rose handed over $315, which she had given to a sixteen-year-old friend to hold for safekeeping.

Delligatta claimed no knowledge of the robbery, but he forked over the $100 the girls had given him for the use of his car. He told interrogators he thought the money was payback for previous damage Rose had done to his vehicle. Upon more questioning, the girls revealed that Delligatta knew why his car was being used.

On May 14, Steven Ray Thomas, Wanda DiCenzi and Rose O'Donnell were indicted on charges of malicious entry of a financial institution and armed robbery. Thomas was held on $10,000 bond. Wanda and Rose were released on $5,000 bond each.

Thomas claimed amnesia before his trial and was referred to the county psychiatric clinic for evaluation. The report declared that he was a sane, intelligent man. "The only clinical explanation for this is conscious deception. We believe he is able to cooperate in his defense," it read. Thomas pleaded guilty and was sentenced to the Ohio State Penitentiary for ten to twenty-five years.

Left to right: Steven Ray Thomas, Rose Therese O'Donnell and Wanda DiCenzi, suspects in the robbery. *Cleveland Public Library.*

Right: Cuyahoga County prosecutor John T. Corrigan. *Cleveland Public Library.*

Below: Cleveland police detectives identified the robbery suspects by viewing film from the surveillance camera. *Cleveland Police Museum.*

Delligatta's name was on the original indictment but was stricken from it. The grand jury foreman checked the jury's vote on Delligatta and found it had returned a no-bill, so Delligatta was removed from the indictment. The police protested to County Prosecutor John T. Corrigan saying Delligatta had supplied the getaway car and the gun. In the fall, Delligatta was finally indicted for receiving stolen property, and he went on trial in late September. Wanda and Rose testified against him. He was found guilty and placed on probation for five years. The girls were also placed on probation.

Years later, records showed Thomas married twice in Indiana. On the morning of December 20, 1967, he was found lying on a sidewalk in Marion, Indiana. He had died during a grand mal seizure. Rose passed away in 2015. Both Delligatta and Wanda moved out of Ohio.

News of the crime-fighting camera kept would-be robbers away from Cleveland banks for more than a year.

6
KARPIS'S MAIL TRUCK AND TRAIN ROBBERIES

B y the end of January 1935, the most notorious gangsters and killers were either in the big house or six feet under. Dillinger had been gunned down outside the Biograph movie theater in Chicago. A hail of lead brought "Pretty Boy" Floyd to the ground in a cornfield outside of East Liverpool. Bonnie and Clyde died when lawmen ambushed their stolen Ford Deluxe in Bienville Parish, Louisiana. Freddy and Arizona Kate "Ma" Barker died in a four-hour shootout with the FBI in Ocklawaha, Florida. Arthur R. "Doc" (rarely "Dock") Barker fared better than his brother and mother, as he was arrested without incident on a Chicago street. More than a dozen people witnessed "Baby Face" Nelson's last stand in Barrington, Illinois, where he was shot nine times by FBI. And Al Capone was sitting in a jail cell at Alcatraz—not for murder but for income tax evasion.

With all these gangsters out of commission, Alvin "Creepy" Karpis found himself promoted to the number one spot on J. Edgar Hoover's Public Enemy list. The brown-haired, blue-eyed hoodlum picked up the "Creepy" nickname along the way. It was sometimes said he got the moniker because of his sinister smile and cold stare, but he told author Robert Livesey in *On the Rock: Alvin Karpis, Public Enemy Number One* that it came from a police officer who was chasing him and lost him. The cop thought it was creepy how evasive Karpis could be.

Francis Albin Karpovicz was raised in Topeka, Kansas, but he was born in Montreal, Canada, to Lithuanian immigrants on August 10, 1907. He started out as a two-bit hood but quickly climbed the criminal ladder when he fell in with the Barker gang. Articulate, smart and cunning, he made a name for himself in the early 1930s when he and Fred Barker robbed banks throughout the Midwest. Even more brazen, the Karpis-Barker Gang pulled off the kidnappings of brewery president Theodore A. Hamm in 1933 and bank president Edward G. Bremer in 1934.

The spring and summer of 1935 were hot for Karpis—not just from the weather, but from the FBI breathing down his neck. He was wanted for the kidnappings, as well as bank robbery, car theft and murder. Law enforcement put a target on his back after a shootout with police at the Dan-mor Hotel in Atlantic City. Leaving his eight-month-pregnant girlfriend, Delores Delany, behind, he and buddy Harry Campbell escaped from

Alvin "Creepy" Karpis. *Cleveland Press Collection, CSU, Michael Schwartz Library.*

there in a stolen car. After that, police were under orders to shoot to kill him on sight.

Crime ran in Karpis's veins. In *The Alvin Karpis Story*, written with Bill Trent, Karpis wrote that he considered crime his job. In his own words: "My profession was robbing banks, knocking off payrolls and kidnapping rich men. I was good at it." He added, "My work became a profession because that's how I approached it." He claimed he could have been a top lawyer or successful businessman. In his opinion, he could have held a high-up job in law enforcement. "I outthought, outwitted, and just plain defeated enough cops and G-men in my time to recognize that I was more knowledgeable about crime than any of them, including the number-one guy, J. Edgar Hoover of the Federal Bureau of Investigation."

Ohio was a favorite haunt for Karpis. He and Campbell often holed up in a bordello owned by Edith Barry in Toledo. He also liked Cleveland and often visited the vice clubs there. Cleveland police commissioner Eliot Ness swore he would capture Karpis, but the gangster was always one step ahead.

In *The Barker-Karpis Gang: An American Crime Family*, W.D. Smith wrote that Karpis met Freddie Hunter at the Harvard Club in Cleveland. A *Cleveland Plain Dealer* reporter called Hunter a small, skinny man with stooped shoulders. According to the *Akron Beacon Journal*, Hunter, a gambler from Warren, proved valuable to Karpis when he tipped him off to a big payroll

Above: Karpis (*right*) and Larry O'Keefe in a 1930 Kansas City arrest. *Acme Newspictures Inc., Cleveland Press Collection, CSU, Michael Schwartz Library.*

Opposite, top: Harry Campbell. *National Archives at San Francisco.*

Opposite, bottom: Early Karpis mug shot. *National Archives at San Francisco.*

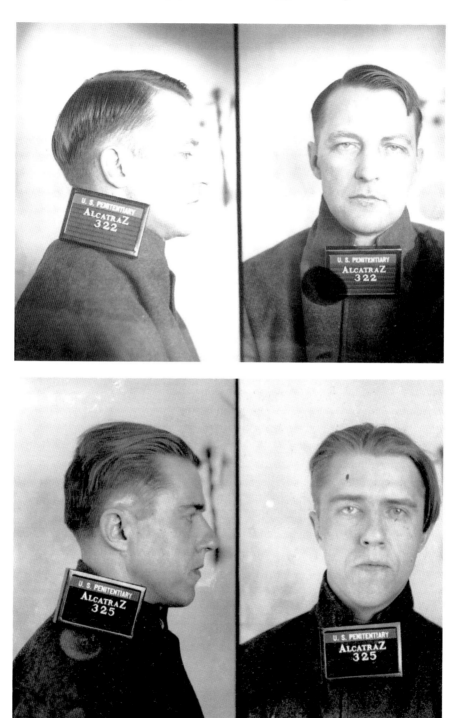

WANTED

$1200.00 REWARD

KATE "MA" BARKER   ARTHUR "DOC" BARKER   FRED BARKER   ALVIN "CREEPY" KARPIS

KARPIS BARKER GANG

KATE "MA" BARKER, AGE 50'S, HEIGHT 5'3", WEIGHT 165 LBS, HAIR DYED BLACK, EYES BROWN
ALVIN 'CREEPY" KARPIS, AGE 22, HEIGHT 5'9", WEIGHT 133 LBS, HAIR BROWN, EYES BLUE
ARTHUR "DOC" BARKER, AGE 25, 5'6", WEIGHT 128 LBS, HAIR BLACK, EYES BROWN
FRED BARKER, AGE 28, HEIGHT 5'4", WEIGHT 115 LBS, LIGHT BROWN, EYES BLUE

MURDER - BANK ROBBERY - KIDNAPPING

WANTED FOR THE MURDER IN "COLD BLOOD'" OF C. R. KELLY SHERIFF OF HOWELL
COUNTY, MISSOURI. THE GANG IS ALSO WANTED FOR THE KIDNAPPINGS OF
WILLIAM HAMM AND EDWARD BREMER. ALONG WITH BEING SUSPECTS IN
SEVERAL ARMED BANK ROBBERIES.

THE GANG SHOULD BE CONSIDERED "EXTREMELY DANGEROUS"

IF YOU HAVE INFORMATION ON THE KARPIS BARKER GANG CONTACT YOUR
LOCAL AUTHORITIES OR
THE UNITED STATES DEPARTMENT OF JUSTICE, DIVISION OF INVESTIGATION.

ISSUED BY FEDERAL BUREAU OF INVESTIGATION   J. EDGAR HOOVER, DIRECTOR

Wanted poster of the Barker Gang. *Author's collection.*

shipment due by train into the Warren post office bound for the Youngstown Sheet and Tube Plant.

The information intrigued Karpis, and in April 1935, he got busy and devised a plan to hijack the mail truck on its route from the post office to the factory. For his plan to work, he needed two other men, so he chose

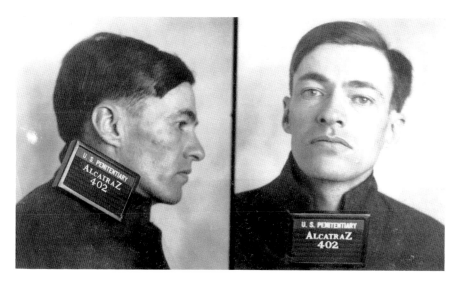

Freddie Hunter. *National Archives at San Francisco.*

Campbell and Hunter's friend drug addict Joe Rich. Karpis studied the mail truck route, so he knew where the best place was to hit it. His plan ran into a couple of snafus: Campbell and Rich got spooked when the driver, Burl Viller, and a station employee looked at them suspiciously at the depot and Campbell saw a black cat cross in front of their vehicle. Karpis drove around for a bit until Campbell and Rich settled down.

By the time they got back to the station, Viller had already pulled the mail truck out onto the street and lost them, so Karpis drove around until he spotted the truck. "I had studied the truck's regular route and I knew, for instance, that it stopped for a certain railway crossing."

Author Wendy Koile wrote in her book *Legends and Lost Treasure of Northern Ohio* that at about 2:30 p.m., the mail truck stopped at that crossing, just as Karpis figured. When it started up again, Karpis pulled the dark green sedan across Pine Street, forcing Viller to hit the brakes. Campbell and Rich leaped out of the car, pistols drawn, and walked over to the truck. Faced with two .45s pointing at him, Viller tossed his own gun out the window and held his hands up.

A couple of young girls happened to come along, just as the gun flew out the window. One of them saw it. She grabbed it up and took off. Karpis was sure she was on her way to the police station a block away.

Campbell and Rich instructed Viller to follow Karpis's car, and he did not argue. They drove down a dirt road on the outskirts of Warren to

Viller's mail truck route. Karpis hijacked the truck at the X. The Warren Police station was at no. 2. The fire department was at no. 1. *Cleveland Press Collection, CSU, Michael Schwartz Library.*

an abandoned garage and pulled in. Viller opened the back of the truck without much prodding, and Karpis and his buddies took possession of the four heavy money bags and loaded them into their car. After tying up Viller and locking him in the back of the mail truck, they pulled out of the garage with $72,000 in cash and $53,000 in bonds. They drove to a deserted garage where they met Hunter and divvied up the cash. The bonds were too hard to negotiate, so they wound up floating in Portage Lakes near Akron and were found three days later.

Police located the mail truck and Viller in short order. George Sargent and Tony Larrizetti, members of the Licavoli mob, were quickly collared for the job. Both had solid alibis, but that did not matter to police. They were well known to authorities, and their rap sheets were yards long. They were convicted for the robbery. Although the prosecutor wanted them in prison, they did their time in the Cuyahoga County Jail. Two years later, Sargent and Larrizetti were freed after evidence came to light that the job was pulled by Karpis.

Akron and Warren detectives inspect the money found in the Portage Lakes. *Cleveland Press Collection, CSU, Michael Schwartz Library.*

In *The Alvin Karpis Story*, the gangster explained how he got the idea of holding up a train from stories he had read about the Wild West. "I was going to take a mail train," he wrote. "I thought of the great bandits of the old West, the James Brothers, the Dalton Boys, and all the rest of them. They knocked over trains, and I was going to pull the same stunt."

After much consideration, he locked focus on Erie Mail Train No. 626, the same one that had carried the payrolls to the post office in Warren where he and his cohorts had hijacked the mail truck in April. "The one I had my eye on was a mail train that carried payrolls from the Federal Reserve Bank in Cleveland to small Ohio towns. It deserved to be taken," he reasoned, "because on payroll day it carried cash enough to cover the weekly salaries of workers in all the giant mills of Youngstown and the other industrial mills." It was the Republic Steel Corporation's payroll for the workers in the Mahoning Valley steel mills. He figured the job could net even more than the kidnappings.

It took him weeks to case the train. Finally, he decided the best place to hit it would be the small Erie Railroad depot at Garrettsville. He was meticulous when planning any robbery, but this one was special. Every last detail had to be perfect. He went over the scheme again and again, looking for any flaws. The best part would be the escape because it would involve an airplane.

Next, Karpis chose his accomplices for their experience. His old pal Harry Campbell would be in on it, and so would Freddie Hunter. Fifty-year-old Benson Groves a.k.a. Ben Grayson was just out of prison for a post office job. Sam Coker had some jobs under his belt and was out of jail on parole thanks to Karpis paying off a crooked politician. John Brock was new, but he came highly recommended by Karpis's friend George "Burrhead" Keady. Brock had been the guest of the Oklahoma State Pen at McAlester.

On Thursday, November 7, 1935, when Erie Railroad Train No. 626 ground to a halt at 2:15 p.m.—two minutes late—Karpis and his bandits, armed with machine guns, automatic pistols and a sawed-off shotgun, stepped out of a new Plymouth sedan and onto the station platform at the Garrettsville depot and took up their positions.

Plain Dealer accounts told of six robbers, but Karpis claimed there were only five. Coker, who was originally assigned to watch the money bags being loaded at the Federal Reserve in Cleveland, was out of commission. According to *The Barker-Karpis Gang: An American Family*, after getting out

Karpis held up an Erie train in 1935 at the Garrettsville Station. *Cleveland Press Collection, CSU, Michael Schwartz Library.*

of prison, Coker made the rounds of Tulsa whorehouses and contacted gonorrhea. He thought he could cure it with iodine injections but wound up in the hospital instead. Karpis thought about replacing him at the last minute but then decided against it.

Witnesses said two of the men wore masks. One wore a black silk handkerchief over the upper part of his face. The other had a white handkerchief over the lower part of his face and glasses covering his eyes. This one could have been Karpis, as he sometimes wore glasses.

According to Karpis, Ben Grayson showed up for the job in a comical disguise of a droopy moustache and rouge on his cheeks. "He looked like a complete villain," Karpis wrote. Having just been released from prison, Grayson wanted to be certain no one recognized him. According to Karpis, two linemen up on a telephone pole pointed to Grayson and began to laugh. "He looked weird as hell."

Disguise or not, Grayson got the drop on engineer Charles Shull and fireman P.O. Leuschner once the train stopped. He ordered them down from the cab, kept them close to the engine and under cover of a gun.

The station agent, William B. Moses, and an Erie telephone lineman, Carl Clutter, were both inside the freight office, according to a *Cleveland Plain Dealer* report. Suddenly one of the robbers—most likely John Brock—appeared in the office window, brandishing a machine gun. "Get outside. Get outside quick or I'll shoot," he snarled at them. Clutter complied, but Moses slammed the door and locked it, then hid in a corner.

Mrs. W.L. Scott, a Garrettsville resident, was at the station to post a letter to her husband. She got the surprise of her life when she heard "Stick 'em up" behind her. She turned to look down the barrel of an automatic pistol. Earl N. Davis, a Garrettsville news agent, thought it was some kind of joke when he heard the order from over his shoulder. He turned to find that it was no joke. A gun was pointed straight at him. Station cashier Fred Ball was up on the truck unloading mail and packages when one of the robbers waved a machine gun at him and ordered him to get down and line up with the others. Scott, Davis, Ball and anyone else around were quickly lined up on the platform and made to hold their hands high in the air.

Karpis saved the starring role in this production for himself. He stepped out of their shiny new getaway car wearing a topcoat with the pocket ripped out. Slung over his shoulder underneath the coat was a machine gun fitted with his preferred twenty-shot clip. He also brought along a couple of dynamite sticks—just in case. He pulled up his 5 feet, 9¾ inches and confidently strode to the mail car, swung his gun from under his coat and leveled at the clerks in the car. He ordered them to throw their hands up. Much to his surprise, they did not raise their hands but dashed back into the dark mail car. Karpis had not counted on this degree of resistance, especially since he was holding a machine gun. He pulled out a stick of dynamite. Just as he was about to toss it into the car, he glanced over and saw that Freddie Hunter had taken off after a couple of tramps who were running down the track. He was supposed to be keeping an eye on the parking lot.

The next thing Karpis knew, a car engine started. He whirled toward the sound. It came from the parking lot a few yards away. He saw a man and woman trying to escape in a car. If they got away, the whole thing could fall apart. Karpis made his decision quickly and ran to the car. Flinging open the driver's door, he yelled, "Get the hell out of the car." He reached in, ripped the keys from the ignition and hurled them across the parking lot.

Karpis dashed back to the platform, but the mail clerks still had not shown their faces. He lobbed an unlighted dynamite stick into the mail car. That failed to flush them out. He threatened to light a second stick and started to count to five. That threat worked, and three mail clerks emerged from the back of the car. Karpis had thought there were only two. Two of the clerks were white. The third clerk Karpis described as a defiant, heavyset Black man. "He was a nervy son-of-a-bitch," Karpis wrote. And not one of the three would put his hands up.

According to Karpis, he tried to fire a shot over their heads, but the gun did not go off. He claimed the sound of the hammer scared them enough, and they finally raised their hands. This was contrary to what Ball told the newspapers. One report claimed that one of the clerks was slightly grazed in the forehead. "I heard a shot fired in the mail car," the station cashier said. "It was only a shot to frighten the clerks and was not aimed at anyone so far as I could see."

Karpis asked which one was the chief clerk. An older man stepped forward. Karpis ordered him back into the mail car. The scene inside the car was daunting to Karpis. He was faced with floor-to-ceiling mail sacks, and the clerk showed no inclination to help sort through them. Karpis again trained his gun on the clerk and reminded him that another train was due to come down the track very soon and it would ram into this train. He wrote in his autobiography that he calmly said, "[T]here'll be a lot of people dead….I don't care about that but you might."

At that the clerk relented and hunted out the Warren payroll, which was in a bag with a heavy padlock. "Where's the other sack, the one from the Federal Reserve Bank?" Karpis asked.

"It isn't here."

Karpis did not believe the clerk and threatened him with the gun again. Just then Campbell jumped on the car. Karpis turned to him and told him to look out; he was going to shoot the old guy if he did not give them the Youngstown payroll. The clerk went to his desk and produced his ledger, which proved he had signed for only one payroll shipment. Apparently, the Youngstown payroll had shipped out the day before.

In a fit of anger, Karpis grabbed five more bags of registered mail in hopes that something of value would be in them. He and Hunter then ordered the clerks to load them in the back of the getaway car.

Mrs. Scott told the newspapers that the robbers made the clerks carry the mail bags over to the car. "I saw one of the robbers pick up one of the mail bags. He used only his thumb and index finger and was mighty careful. It looked as if he was being very careful that he didn't get any finger prints on it."

The robbers were careful not to leave fingerprints—except for Karpis, who had no fingerprints. He had had them removed by underworld plastic surgeon Joseph Moran in March 1933. The operation was so successful that many years later Karpis had trouble obtaining a passport to return to his native Canada.

When ordered to carry the mail bags, the clerk balked. "Hey, I'm not going to help you rob the train." With some incentive in the way of a foot in the backside from Hunter, the clerk grabbed the bags. Davis was ordered out of the line to help load the getaway car. As he dumped four of the sacks into their car, he got a glimpse inside and saw two more machine guns and two or three automatic pistols on the floor.

According to Karpis, the whole robbery took only a few minutes, and the passengers were none the wiser.

Apparently, none of the robbers saw a woman get off the train. According to the *Garrettsville Journal*, she ran to the back of the train and headed across the tracks to Allan D. Sheperd's coal yard office. The man in the office notified the telephone operator of the holdup. The operator already knew about the robbery and had notified the Garrettsville marshal. The first alarm had come from a woman visiting a friend who lived near the station.

When the Federal Reserve Bank tallied its losses, Clarence W. Arnold, the assistant deputy governor of the Cleveland bank, told reporters that the train carried $39,500 in currency that was consigned to a Warren bank and $12,450 in securities. He said the robbers took $34,000 but overlooked $5,500 in cash. The money was to be used for payroll for the Republic Steel

Corporation. Postmaster Michael F. O'Donnell said that six or seven mail pouches were stolen, but only three contained registered mail. One of the bags contained cash on its way to Warren, and the other two contained the securities bound for Pittsburgh. Although the cash money had been stolen, Republic Steel said it would meet its obligation to the works by check.

Karpis knew he could not hide out in Ohio after the robbery, not even at Edith Barry's. The Feds already had an idea he was somewhere in the state even before he knocked over the train. For that reason, the escape was one of the most meticulous he had ever planned. He took great care in his choice of a getaway car. He wanted a four-door Ford with a V8 engine because it had a fast pickup, but there were none to be had in the area. He even offered one car dealer an extra $100 if he could locate one. In the end, he had to settle for the Plymouth.

Karpis and his men sped away in the new car. They headed down a gravel road that eventually joined State Route 80. According to the *Cleveland Plain Dealer*, coal dealer C.P. Morrow followed the car to Freedom Station, and then it turned onto State Route 88 and headed toward Ravenna. Witnesses did manage to get the license number, which came back to an East Side Cleveland address. Police found the house, but it had not been occupied for four months. The car was bought at Knowles-Brown Inc. Plymouth dealers in Cleveland. Russell Brown, owner of the dealership, gave the police the purchaser's name and said he had paid cash for it. The purchaser had a police record. According to Smith's book on the Barker-Karpis gang, Karpis had enlisted Milton Lett to buy the car.

Karpis planned a getaway route that was full of turn backs and twists. He had practiced it so many times before the robbery that he knew every bump in the road. It carried them from Garrettsville north to Port Clinton, where there was a small airport. He was pleased with how well the robbery and their escape had gone. The disappointment set in when they tore open the payroll bag and mail sacks. The haul totaled no more than $34,000. He had expected far more. According to his autobiography, in the end he congratulated himself for pulling off a train robbery "in fine style just like the famous old Western bandits."

Karpis had bought a light Stinson plane and hired a former bootlegger pilot named John Zetzer. The morning after the robbery, Zetzer had the plane warmed up and ready to fly Karpis and Hunter to Hot Springs, Arkansas, and into the arms of their girlfriends there. The trip was a rough one. The plane nearly ran out of fuel twice, and Zetzer was forced to land it near Evansville, Indiana, and again near Memphis, Tennessee. They slept

Karpis's girlfriend Jewell Laverne Grayson, aka Grace Goldstein, was a madam in Hot Springs, Arkansas. *Cleveland Press Collection, CSU, Michael Schwartz Library.*

in the plane overnight in Indiana while Zetzer walked to get gas and slept in a hotel near Memphis. Karpis gave the plane to Zetzer after the trip and forked over an extra $500 to him to get rid of the Plymouth. Zetzer told an *Akron Beacon Journal* reporter that he did not know who his two passengers were.

Karpis had a fondness for prostitutes, particularly madams. He kept company for some time with a bleached blond named Grace Goldstein, a.k.a. Jewel Laverne Grayson. She ran the Hatterie Hotel in Hot Springs and wielded some influence over the town big shots. After the train robbery, the two took off on vacation to Florida. She claimed to have married Karpis in September 1935 in New York, but no documents were ever found to back up that claim.

On May 1, 1936, as Karpis and Hunter were walking to Hunter's car on Canal Street near an apartment where Karpis was staying in New Orleans, they were arrested by the FBI. Karpis said several agents swarmed them with guns. He caught sight of Hoover lurking around the corner of the apartment building. When the scene was under control, Hoover came out from behind the building. None of the agents had handcuffs. In an interview later in life, Karpis claimed that they used his own striped necktie to bind his hands. However, Special Agent W.L. "Buck" Buchanan claimed it was his own and sent it to Hoover as a memento.

One of Karpis's brothers-in-law was of the opinion that one of the gangster's friends had tipped authorities off about his whereabouts. Sylvester J. Hettrick, the post office inspector in Cleveland, said, "I'm not supposed to talk," when he was asked if it was John Brock who had ratted Karpis out.

Karpis was flown from warm New Orleans weather to cold St. Paul in light-weight clothes and a straw hat. He shivered as he got off the small plane. He was brought to trial there. At first, he pleaded not guilty to kidnapping charges. A few weeks later he agreed to plead guilty to conspiracy if the kidnapping charges were dropped. The court accepted his offer. He was incarcerated at Alcatraz for twenty-six years and was the longest-serving

Above: Hoover is in the foreground as Karpis is led into a St. Paul courtroom. *Acme Newspictures Inc., Cleveland Press Collection, CSU, Michael Schwartz Library.*

Right: Karpis's official mug shot after his capture in New Orleans. *Cleveland Press Collection, CSU, Michael Schwartz Library.*

Right: Karpis (*right*), shown with his attorney, James Carty, was deported to Canada upon release from prison. *Acme Newspictures Inc., Cleveland Press Collection, CSU, Michael Schwartz Library.*

Below: Young Karpis was considered a public enemy. An older Karpis was paroled after thirty-three years. *Cleveland Press Collection, CSU, Michael Schwartz Library.*

prisoner on that island. He did six months at Leavenworth Prison during a short term. When Alcatraz closed in 1962, he was sent to McNeil Island Penitentiary in Washington State.

After thirty-three years in various prisons, he was paroled and deported to Canada. Three years later, he moved to Torremolinos, Spain, where he died of heart failure on August 26, 1979, according to Livesey. He was buried in niche grave no. 2300 in the Cementerio de San Miguel in Malaga, Spain. When the lease for the niche expired, with no one to claim his body, his remains were removed and reinterred in a communal grave in the mountains as was Spanish custom.

7

GRAVE CONCERNS

During the eighteenth and nineteenth centuries, medical schools paid body snatchers—sometimes called resurrection men—to dig up freshly buried corpses to be used for dissection or anatomy lessons.

Desecrating graves was illegal and usually done under cover of darkness, but it was a lucrative business. The graves of paupers, African Americans, orphans, transients and the insane buried in potters' fields were the most common graves to be robbed because they were less likely to be guarded. More affluent families hired guards to watch over their loved ones' graves and used iron coffins, fences or wire cages to protect from body snatching.

When John Scott Harrison of North Bend, Ohio, was interred at the Congress Green Cemetery, his family not only hired a guard for thirty dollars for thirty nights, but they also had the tomb walled in brick and the coffin covered with stone slabs and cement. As solid as those deterrents were, they were not enough to keep his body from being dug up, stripped naked and hung by the neck with a windlass in a shaft at the Medical School of Ohio in Cincinnati.

The Honorable John Scott Harrison was the son of President William Henry Harrison (ninth), the father of President Benjamin Harrison (twenty-third) and the grandson of Benjamin Harrison V, a signer of the Declaration of Independence. Harrison was a Democratic member of the United States House of Representatives from the First Ohio Congressional District from 1853 to 1857.

Illustration of resurrectionists at their ghoulish work. *Author's collection.*

In the days leading up to his death, the seventy-four-year-old complained of chest pains, but that did not keep him from carrying on his usual duties. On Saturday evening, May 25, 1878, Harrison went to bed at the usual time. On Sunday morning, his grandson (his son and family lived with him) went up to his room to call him to breakfast. He found Harrison lying on the floor partially dressed. No one was certain whether he died before going to bed or whether he had gotten up in the night and dropped dead. A bottle of peppermint was found close by, leading his family to believe the latter.

His funeral was held in the Presbyterian church in Cleves four days later. It was attended by a huge crowd, which included dignitaries. He was laid to rest with his father and the other Harrison dead in the cemetery in North Bend.

While the grave was being readied, Harrison's son John and a grandson, George C. Eaton, noticed the grave of Augustus Devin on a lot close by looked as though it had been disturbed. Newspaper accounts say twenty-three-year-old Devin died of consumption, but a short biography on Find a Grave claims a classmate struck "Gus" in the back and the injury caused a hemorrhage four years later, which led to his death. Devin had been good friends with John and George, so the young Harrisons thought they should check the grave for tampering.

Their suspicion unnerved John Scott Harrison's son General Benjamin Harrison (later President Harrison), and he wanted to make sure his father's grave would not be violated. Before he went home to Indianapolis, he hired T.M. Linn to guard the grave. Linn was a plasterer and stonemason who helped dig the grave and cement the brick walls. Linn was supposed to check it once every hour during the night.

After the funeral, John and George inspected Devin's grave and discovered his body was missing. Wanting to save his wife and family any further sadness, they decided to investigate and try to recover the body themselves. Logic told them his body was somewhere within the walls of one of the medical colleges in Cincinnati, so they secured the proper documents to search. Constable Walter Lacy, Deputy Tallen and Colonel Thomas E. Snelbaker accompanied them on their pursuit. The Ohio Medical College was known to receive the most cadavers, so it was their first stop. Founded in 1819 by Daniel Drake, it sat on Sixth Street between Vine and Race.

The janitor, A.Q. Marshall, let them in. They searched the building from top to bottom but did not find Devin's body. As they were getting ready to leave the dissection room, Constable Lacy noticed a heavy beam supporting a windlass over a trapdoor that covered a shaft in the corner of the room. A rope ran down into a shaft. He tested it and found it was pulled taught from the windlass. "Hold on, there may be something on this rope," he said. He pulled open the trapdoors. The rope went far down into the dark shaft. Snelbaker cranked the windlass. Something heavy was at the end of the rope, and it took a great deal of muscle to crank the handle. Finally, after great effort and about ten minutes, the contraption revealed a nude body, its face covered with a white cloth, its arms crossed in front of it, ropes holding them at midsection. It was suspended by the neck.

The body was too well nourished to be young Devin, who was emaciated at death. Gray hair stuck out from under a cloth that covered the cadaver's head.

Dr. William W. Seely, one of the directors, entered the room at that point. He told John and George that since they had not found the body of Augustus Devin, they should say nothing to Mrs. Devin. If she did not know her husband's body had been stolen, she would suffer no more grief.

The young men were happy to let the body back down into the shaft, but Lacy had made up his mind to remove the cloth from the corpse's head. He pulled it off. John and George were aghast at what they saw.

John began to tremble, "It is ———, it is ———."

"It is the body of his father," George said hoarsely.

Both young men broke into sobs as they looked in horror upon the body of John Scott Harrison, who had been laid to rest the day before.

"Well, it will all be the same on the day of resurrection," Dr. Seely said heartlessly.

They laid the body on the floor and gave it a quick examination to make sure it was John Scott Harrison. There was a bruise on the right side of his forehead, matching the one Harrison had suffered when he fell dead. A mole on the forehead also matched one on the deceased. The young men noticed a bloody cut under the chin most likely made when the resurrectionists had pulled him from his grave.

Wailing in grief, John drew a tobacco knife from his pocket and sat down on the floor next to his dead father. He was determined to guard his father while George ran to fetch the undertaker from Estep & Meyer Funeral Parlor on Seventh Street who had buried Harrison. Lacy stayed behind with John and the body. They waited for George and the undertaker for what must have seemed like an eternity. Finally, they took Harrison's body to the funeral home. After a bit, they had the wherewithal to consider checking the grave to make sure it had been robbed.

Carter B. Harrison, who lived at Cleves, was another son of the victim. He had already received information that the grave had been robbed. He telegraphed Benjamin: "Father's grave has been robbed. I shall leave for Cincinnati on the first train. Come there immediately."

The Harrison brothers started their inquiry by talking to Linn, the man hired to watch the grave. He claimed to have visited the grave four times that night, once at 11:00 p.m., again at midnight, then at 2:00 a.m. and finally at daybreak. When he went in the morning, he noticed a difference between the head and foot of the grave. It was not finished off in a mound as it should have been. The dirt at the end should have been patted down, but it was loose. Linn and the gravedigger determined the grave had been tampered with. Linn took a stick and probed in the dirt, looking for some pieces of rock he had placed at the foot of the grave. When he did not find them, he knew the grave had been opened. He and the gravedigger dug down into the earth and found the rocks upended and the pine coffin opened. Auger holes had been bored in a curved line across the lid. The end of the casket was broken off, the foot pried open, so the body had been dragged out feet first.

Linn said it was a skillful job, possibly executed by someone who had been at the funeral or knew someone who was. The culprits knew exactly what tools to bring and how to use them.

Carter suspected the janitor at the medical college, so he went to a justice of the peace and had a warrant sworn out for his arrest. Marshall, a Civil War veteran, was locked up in the county jail. Drs. Seely, Phineas S. Conner and Frederick Forcheimer secured Thomas A. Logan as his attorney. Logan argued Marshall was not likely to know when a body had been brought into the college or by whom. Marshall's bail was set at $5,000.

According to a witness, a buggy with two occupants was seen entering the alley from Vine Street in back of the Medical College around 3:00 a.m. on the evening in question. It pulled up to the door near the chute where bodies were delivered. The occupants took a white object from the buggy and slid it into the chute. Afterward, the buggy drove hurriedly toward Race Street. The Harrison men were certain the buggy delivered their father's corpse to the Medical College.

Benjamin Harrison was so outraged he wrote a letter to the citizens of Cincinnati that was published in the *Cincinnati Daily Gazette*. In part, he wrote, "[K]eep your precious dead from the barbarous touch of the grave robber, and you from that taste of hell which comes with the discovery of a

Benjamin Harrison.
Library of Congress.

father's grave robbed and the body hanging by the neck like that of a dog, in the pit of a medical college."

The future president went on to acknowledge the kindness he and his family had received from the public. He also wanted to fix the blame. "I have no satisfactory evidence that any of them [Medical College faculty] knew whose body they had, but I have the most convincing evidence that they are covering the guilty scoundrel." He was adamant that the doctors of the college were hiding the identities of the resurrection men. "The bodies brought there are purchased and paid for by an officer of the college. The body snatcher stands before him and takes from his hand the fee for his hellish work…He is often there, and it is silly to say that he is unknown."

Marshall, the janitor, was in custody, but he was not talking. He denied knowing the body was there. Benjamin Harrison did not believe him. "[B]ut the clean incision into the carotid artery, the thread with which it was ligatured, the injected veins prove him a liar. Who made the incision and injected the body, gentlemen of the faculty?"

The saddest part of the letter had to do with his father's beard. "While he lay upon your table, the long white beard, which the hands of infant grandchildren had often stroked in love, was rudely shorn from his face."

In conclusion, he asked: "Who took him from that table and hung him by the neck in the pit? Was it to hide it from friends or to pass his body in your pickling vats for fall use?" He went on: "[W]ho drew my father by the feet, through broken glass and dirt from his honored grave?"

In answer to Benjamin Harrison's outrage, Dr. Robert Bartholow, dean of the Ohio Medical College, claimed that "members of the faculty were entirely ignorant of the robbery of the grave of the late John Scott Harrison." The allegation that the body had been stolen for the doctors to ascertain the cause of death was completely false, Bartholow claimed. "It is scarcely necessary to say that the explanation already given is the true one—that a resurrectionist, unknown to us, who was probably short of funds, took this means to replenish his exchequer."

When the matter was brought before the grand jury, Benjamin Harrison hoped to question each member of the faculty, but he did not get that chance. He told authorities that Dr. Seely had sent word to him that he would reveal the name of the body snatcher who had desecrated John Scott Harrison's grave. But when Harrison called on Seely, the doctor refused the information.

Under oath, faculty claimed they did not know who the resurrectionist was. At the time the body came in, none of the members was in the building.

"The faculty is not positive who the resurrectionist was, as there are several employed by them to furnish 'stiffs.'" They denied trying to conceal the body. The faulty admitted that they, as well as other medical colleges, had contracts with resurrectionists to provide them with cadavers for dissection and anatomical demonstration. The contracts stipulated that no private burying grounds should be disturbed, nor should graves of persons with families or friends be molested. The college did not always know where the bodies came from, but if the resurrectionists violated this clause, they were on their own and the college would not protect them.

Part of the contract said the bodies would be placed in the dissecting room. They were also supposed to shave the face of a man with a beard, cut the hair and inject the arteries and veins with a preserving fluid.

Ghoulish drop-offs to the college must have been a common occurrence. Firemen who were on duty at the nearby Gift's Engine House testified that one night they heard the noise of a wagon coming from the alley behind the school. They went out to see what was going on and observed a wagon had stopped in front of the chute near the back door of the college. There was something in the form of a human body covered in blankets and a number of muskets in the bed of the wagon. The firemen said there were three men in the wagon. They followed it up Race Street.

While the Harrison family was making arrangement to reinter John Scott Harrison in the family tomb, Snelbaker continued the hunt for Devin's body. Days later, he obtained a warrant for the Miami Medical College on Twelfth Street near Elm. He, a deputy and a *Cincinnati Enquirer* reporter were met at the door by the janitor. According to the unnamed reporter, the janitor "attempted to appear at ease" as he offered to show searchers the rooms upstairs. But Snelbaker was more interested in the cellar and wanted to look there first. The janitor became very nervous at that point but lighted a lamp and led him down the steps. Although the detective made a thorough search of the cellar, checking every box and barrel, he came away with nothing.

"I know that this body was buried in the cellar of this college last Thursday, and I have my doubts if it is not down there yet," Snelbaker said. "Come now, I don't care if you have forty bodies here, if you will turn up Devin's body I will make no further search."

The janitor (who was never named in any of the newspaper articles) was clearly rattled when Snelbaker said he would dig up every inch of the cellar if he had to. Finally, the janitor relented. "Suppose I tell you that the body you are after is not here, but that I can put you onto the track of it."

"Very well," Snelbaker said. "If you do, it will save you a heap of trouble and may be the means of preventing your arrest."

The janitor told Snelbaker that a resurrectionist named Gabriel had come to him claiming to have permission from Dr. William Clendenin, dean of the college and professor of anatomy, to use the cellar to store "stiffs," then prepare them to be shipped to Ann Arbor, Michigan. "Gabriel" brought a number of bodies to the college and the janitor thought Devin might have been one of them. He went on to say that thirteen bodies had been put in boxes and barrels and shipped by American Express to J.Q. Quimby & Co. in Ann Arbor. Snelbaker suspected the bodies had come from several different cemeteries in and around Cincinnati. When John Scott Harrison's body was discovered at the Ohio Medical College, it caused a great deal of excitement, and Gabriel skipped town bound for Canada.

Gabriel sometimes went by the name Dr. Christian a.k.a. Dr. Gordon a.k.a. Charles O. Morton. His real name was Dr. Henri Le Caron. He began robbing graves as a medical student to pay his tuition at the Detroit Medical College. He and three others, Henry Morton, Morton's brother and Thomas Beverly a.k.a. Johnson, had a regular business in grave robbing, at one point filling an order for seventy cadavers.

Le Caron had fallen into the clutches of police in Toledo the previous January when he was caught with the bodies of an eighty-three-year-old woman and a thirteen-year-old boy. While he was in jail, some of his medical friends smuggled in a vial of croton oil, which La Caron applied to his skin. It caused hideous eruptions that looked like smallpox. The board of health immediately had him removed from jail and taken to the "pest house" (a hospital for patients suffering from infectious diseases). He escaped from the hospital while his guards were having supper.

Snelbaker went to American Express and obtained a list of the shipments to J.Q. Quimby & Co. The list in hand, he started for Ann Arbor the next day. The first thing he found was that J.Q. Quimby & Co. did not exist. Instead, it was a blind for the medical department of the Michigan State University. Accompanied by Sheriff Josiah S. Case, Snelbaker approached the college with a warrant. They were granted entrance in the evening of June 14. Devin's brother Bernard and George Eaton had described Devin in detail, including his scars.

As two medical students opened the pickling vat and pulled out the corpses, Snelbaker scrutinized each one and decided on three that looked as if they could be Augustus Devin. He then sent for Bernard and George. They arrived around eight o'clock in the evening and immediately went to the college.

John Scott Harrison was buried in the Harrison family tomb. *Ohio History Connection.*

They were escorted into a dark "little pent-up apartment in the basement." The walls were stacked with old coffins, barrels and trunks. A sickening odor emanated from two vats. Two medical students, B.L. Evans and M.S. Pasco, donned rubber aprons and gloves before pulling out the three corpses.

Bernard identified the second as his brother, Augustus Devin, by a little hole in the wall of his nose, the decayed front teeth, a moustache and a scar on his leg. The demonstrator of anatomy, Professor W.J. Herdman, required them to sign an affidavit as to the identity of the body and agreed to prepare it for shipment to North Bend.

In the morning, when Devin's brothers went to take custody of the body, Evans and Pasco refused to release it unless Bernard paid them thirty dollars. He flatly refused and threatened legal action. The president and faculty of the Ann Arbor college ordered the body to be released.

Bernard and George left Ann Arbor for Cincinnati the next morning with the remains of Augustus Devin. At home, they were met at the depot by a crowd of 150 people, including the Harrisons.

After this ghoulish crime, the citizens of North Bend formed a guard at the cemetery. Well-armed men were stationed at different points among the graves at night.

The grand jury refused to indict the faculty of the medical college. Benjamin Harrison filed suit against the college. The outcome of that case, as well as the criminal case against Marshall, is not known. In 1884, a fire destroyed the Hamilton County Courthouse and all criminal and civil case records were lost.

8
ALL THAT GLITTERS

My first few scores were for money. I mean I needed money when I was young," Bill Mason told Brett Ratner, director of *Prison Break*, *Rush Hour* and others during an "Interview with a Jewel Thief" on YouTube (undated). "After that, they [the thefts] slowly but surely became adrenaline rushes."

In 2003, when Mason's crimes were well out of the statute of limitations, he collaborated with author Lee Gruenfeld on *Confessions of a Master Jewel Thief* about his capers in Ohio and Florida. The handsome and charming thief stole $35 million worth of precious jewelry in his career.

William Michael Mason was born in Hundred, West Virginia, in August 1940, the only child of Ella and Ora Mason, two teachers. The family moved to Shaker Heights after the war sunk Hundred's and surrounding Monongalia County's economy.

When Bill was old enough, he began helping Ora with the apartment buildings he managed. Bill learned from repairmen and tradesmen, but he was most interested in locks and security systems.

Bill found his way into crime after a night out with an old school chum who worked at a miniature golf course. The friend mentioned the owner made money—all cash—hand over fist. He told Bill the owner stashed the loot away in a safe in the concession stand.

In the following days, the conversation kept creeping into Bill's thoughts. He admitted in his book to taking his wife and daughter to the miniature golf course every weekend to have a look around and "exercise" his imagination.

He went to the concession stand and laid eyes on the safe right behind the counter. Although he knew nothing about safecracking, this one looked like a piece of junk. How hard could it be? He tried to think of every obstacle and a way around it. He related how the job went in his book and in the interview with Ratner.

The night he decided to act, he parked at a motel a quarter mile up the road from the golf course and went down through a ravine that paralleled the road. Because he was a novice at safecracking, he carried every tool he thought he might need—power tools, a sledgehammer, a drill, a saw, even a flatbed dolly. He snipped the concession stand lock with his bolt cutters, got inside and went to work. He wedged a chisel in between the door and the frame and pounded it with his sledgehammer, loosening the door somewhat but not enough. He broke two expensive drill bits trying to drill it open. He used a rotary saw, hoping it would gnaw through the steel, but that just chewed up two blades. He went after it with two different crowbars but only succeeded in bending them.

After two hours of smashing, drilling, prying and pounding on the steel and cement safe, he realized he needed heavier tools. After spending all that time and muscle, he was not going to let it beat him. "Then I tried to haul it away," he told Ratner in the interview.

He tipped the three-hundred-pound safe onto the dolly, scooped up his tools and wheeled everything outside. The dolly rolled fine on the cement walkway, but the wheels would not budge in the soft ground. He gave the safe a mighty shove to get it off the dolly and then put his strength into flipping it end over end, stopping every so often to catch his breath and to look around and listen. "It took me all night trying to get it out of there."

Bill lost control of it at the top of the ravine. It thundered down into the water and came to rest in the mud.

He slid down the hill after it and commenced pushing it out of the sucking mud. It took every bit of his strength, but he was determined. He managed to roll the three-hundred-pound behemoth up the side of the creek bed.

Just as day broke, he brought his car to the safe. "Then I couldn't get it in the trunk," he told Ratner.

Bill was inventive if nothing else. He unbolted the front seat of the car and tossed it into the back and maneuvered the safe into the driver's side. "I rode sitting on the safe."

The next morning, he used an acetylene torch and cut the door off. Water and mud had seeped in through the seams as he dragged it through the ravine. The five grand inside was soaked and covered with mud. He washed it in the shower and stuck all $5,000 of it to the walls to dry. He loaded the safe into his car and drove it to a lake, where he dumped it.

From the way he told it in his *Confessions of a Master Jewel Thief*, he moved way up with his next score. Big time. Really big time. He set his sights on a safe belonging to Angelo "Big Ange" Lonardo, the underboss of the Cleveland Mob.

Lonardo owned the Highlander, a hotel, super club and posh key club on Northfield Road in Warrensville Heights. The key club was most exclusive. Bill was not a member, but he was good-looking and well dressed, so he managed to slip in.

Having made friends with a waitress at the supper club, Bill got her talking after hours one night. She told him about a high-class gambling den that "Big Ange" and his nephew "Little Ange" ran. After that conversation, Bill looked up a tenant in a building he managed. The guy was a drunk, and Bill knew he gambled. If anyone knew about Lonardo's gambling den, it was this tenant. Bill learned from him that Lonardo's was a high-stakes place.

Bill could not just walk in. He did not have that kind of money to gamble, so he would never blend in. Instead, he watched the place from a half a block down the street. He saw people who were dressed to the nines go through the doors. They looked like they could drop a bundle and not bat an eye.

Saturday nights were the busiest. The club closed at 3:00 a.m., and Little Ange came out carrying a black bag. Bill figured it was full of money, so he tailed him back to the Highlander, where Little Ange went up to the second floor to the office, Bill sneaking behind. He noted the maid's supply room on one side of the office and a guest room on the other. The laundry room was on the first floor right underneath the office.

Little Ange swiped a card in the lock, opened the door and punched in a code on an alarm panel. The alarm was a problem, Bill wrote. A security guard wandered the halls, and that was another problem.

Bill took a month to plan. During that time, he and his wife had dinner and stayed the night at the Highlander, giving Bill more opportunity to case. He found that the walls of the hotel room were exceedingly thin. That gave him the idea to cut through the drywall of the room beside the office instead of dealing with the alarm. He also discovered that the security guard took naps at night when no one was around. That brought it to July 4, which was bound to be a lucrative evening.

A few days before his target date, an elderly couple rented the room next to the office. Bill's whole plan could go down the drain if they did not move out. But he got an idea. When the couple went out to dinner, he slipped into the room—the lock was no problem. He loosened a nut on the sink pipe in the bathroom and turned on the faucet. He let the carpet get soaked and then retightened the nut just enough so water still dripped. It worked. The couple got moved to another room.

Bill knew stealing from the mob was risky. Jail would be a holiday if the police caught him compared to what the mob would do. With the mob, he would end up on the bottom of Lake Erie. But he decided the risk was worth it. "I knew there was a lot of money in there," he said. "And I figured I could get away with it."

Leading up to the job, he assembled the tools of his trade: sledgehammer, chisels, cutting torch, high-speed drill and a portable hydraulic jack, which he bought specifically for this job.

That night, Little Ange made the drop at the second-floor office just after 3:00 a.m. Bill let himself into the hotel room next to the office and cut through the wall into the office using a drywall knife. He slid between the studs. The safe was right in front of him. He laid out his tools. As he twisted to take a look at the hinges of the safe, he lost his balance and grabbed the safe handle to steady himself. To his amazement, the handle went down and the safe opened. Little Ange had not locked it. The black bag full of money was there. And so were stacks of more cash and jewelry. He grabbed the jewelry first, then the money, and shoved it all into his carryall. He squeezed everything back through the hole in the wall, dragged it quietly down the hall and outside to his car. The whole job took less than an hour.

The next day, he counted his take. It was at least $100,000. The police were not notified, and the papers never reported the theft. A police report and investigation were made after Bill stole a quarter of a million dollars' worth of jewelry from comedienne and Lima native Phyllis Diller.

Bill had seen Diller interviewed on the Cleveland morning TV's *Mike Douglas Show*. She was loaded down with jewelry, and Bill wondered if it was real. Newspapers revealed that she was coming to the Musicarnival, a tent theater in the round in Warrenville Heights. Bill bought a ticket hoping to get a closer look at her jewelry. He attended two shows and followed her limousine after the second show to the Blue Grass, a restaurant celebrities favored when in town. Two big hulks escorted her to a table, so Bill took up a position at the bar where he could keep an eye on her.

When she and her bodyguards left the restaurant, Bill followed their limousine to the Highlander. He scouted around a bit and found that her whole entourage took up an entire floor, but he was not sure which room was hers. The next day, he appeared at the Highlander in work clothes, a

Phyllis Diller lost her jewelry to Bill Mason while she was performing at Musicarnival. *Cleveland Press Collection, CSU, Michael Schwartz Library.*

cap and sunglasses and carrying a clipboard and tape measure. No one paid any attention to him because they assumed he was there working. He went to Diller's floor and pretended to measure something and scribbled on his clipboard. Lucky for him, a bell clerk with a food cart knocked on a door and Diller—no makeup and wearing a ratty old bathrobe—answered.

Bill saw a balcony and sliding glass doors leading into her suite. To get to her balcony, he needed to get up on the roof so he could lower himself down on a rope. Both doors leading to the roof were secured with combination locks. He took down the make and numbers of the locks and then, using stationery from one of the buildings he managed, wrote to the manufacturer, claiming he had lost the combinations. The manufacturer wrote back with the magic numbers.

The night after he received the combination, he donned his work uniform of all black and packed his carryall with rope and tools. He pulled on his black gloves and headed out for the Highlander and Phyllis Diller's jewels.

When Bill was sure Diller was safely in her limousine and on the way to the Musicarnival, he went to work. He unlocked the roof door to the wing of the hotel opposite her room, stuck a toothpick in the doorknob, so it wouldn't open from the inside, and climbed onto the roof. From there, he could see her room. He used the binoculars to watch the room to be sure no one had stayed behind.

After an hour of no movement in the room, Bill went over to the wing where her room was. Once on the roof of that wing, he anchored his rope around a vent stack. After another ten minutes of watching and listening, he took hold of the rope and lowered himself to Diller's balcony. Music was coming from her room. That made him nervous. He waited. Nothing happened. Cautiously, he opened the sliding glass door and stepped inside. Satisfied he was alone, he looked around. The room was in chaos— clothing and towels thrown around and dirty dishes everywhere. In spite of the mess, he saw the jewelry box in a half-open bureau drawer. It was crammed full of gold and gemstones. He shoved all of it into his bag and left the way he came in.

According to Bill, the next day's paper reported Diller had lost a quarter of a million dollars in jewelry. One unforgettable piece was a Cartier watch inscribed on the back, "Love to Phyllis from Bob Hope." He replaced the back with a new one and melted down the inscribed one with some other pieces. He waited ten years before taking the jewelry to New York to a Madison Avenue store and leaving it on consignment. No one asked questions. The pieces sold to a European buyer.

In 1972, Bill moved his family to Fort Lauderdale, Florida—the ideal area for a cat burglar. The beach was lined with skyscraper condos and hotels inhabited by wealthy people with loads of money and jewelry. According to a 1985 *Plain Dealer* article by Madeline Drexler and James Neff, south Florida police caught him twice and estimated he had committed at least one hundred break-ins. Bill was looking at some serious time after his second arrest, so he fled back to Shaker Heights and borrowed the identity of a willing friend.

On St. Patrick's Day, Bill met Francine Kravitz Loveman at the Ground Floor, a Shaker Heights bar. He became enthralled with her, and she with him. She was the daughter of a wealthy family that owned grocery chains and the wife of a rich engineer. Newspapers called her a socialite. Bill had strained his marriage to the breaking point, and Francine wanted change. They eventually divorced their spouses and moved in together in a house in Moreland Hills.

One day in July 1980, Bill overheard Fran talking with friends about a party they had attended the night before. Bill's ears perked up when he heard about the jewelry Florence Mandel, another guest at the party, had worn. Florence was the wife of Joseph Mandel, the co-founder and chairman of Premier Industrial Corporation. Bill became even more interested when someone talked about Florence's golf ball–sized ring.

The Mandels were one of the most prominent and wealthy families in Cleveland. They lived in Acacia on the Green, an exclusive and secure apartment complex in Lyndhurst. Bill tucked that information away for later use.

Planning a jewel heist was an adrenaline rush. "Putting the puzzle together was part of it. I became addicted," he told Ratner.

Bill's plans were always meticulous. Bill wrote that the public library was his first stop to get the Mandels' phone number and unit address. His next

Francine Kravitz
Loveman and Bill Mason.
From the Plain Dealer.

step was a visit to the county building office to look up the construction plans for the complex. He said when he cased a place, he "always looked for the flaws in their security systems."

When he went to look at Acacia on the Green, he found the complex was off Cedar Road and backed up by a golf course. It consisted of two sand-colored brick buildings, each with wings out to the side and to the back. From the street, they appeared to be six stories high.

Bill drove a van with blacked-out windows. He pulled into a spot across the street where he could sit and observe for a while. There was a gate across the driveway but no fences around the property. Nights later, he paid another visit. This time he walked onto the grounds for a closer look. The exterior doors were monitored by cameras.

Bill wanted to have a look inside, so the next night, he slicked his hair back, shaved and donned a well-tailored but nondescript business suit. Concealed by the shadows, he waited outside the gate until a group a people showed up, then walked in with them unnoticed.

Bill rode the elevator to the top floor and walked around until he saw Mandel's name on one of the doors. He paced off the footage from the door to the windows on the side of the building. That way, he could gauge which condo it was from the outside.

Bill checked the door leading to the roof. It was unlocked. He climbed up to the roof and began to pace off what he thought would be the footage to the Mandels' apartment. He peered down over the side of the building for their balcony and saw the atrium. It opened

Joseph Mandel. *Cleveland Press Collection, CSU, Michael Schwartz Library.*

right into the Mandels' apartment. The only impediment was a sliding glass door. No problem.

Bill went home that night, knowing all he had to do was pick the right time. Luck was on his side. Fran's parents were friends with the Mandels. She mentioned the four of them were going out to dinner the following Tuesday evening. That gave Bill a few days to gather his gear.

The first thing he needed was a scanner to monitor police activity. He bought a portable, light-weight unit and fashioned a shoulder harness for under his arm. He also bought a book with police frequencies. He plugged a wire into the scanner and ran it under his shirt up to his ear so he could hear if police had detected his activity in the Mandel apartment. He put fresh batteries in it and tested it to make sure it worked properly.

On September 23, 1980, he suited up with the scanner strapped under his arm and the wire attached. He wound a rope around his waist and slid his arms into an expensive leather jacket to cover the rope and the scanner. He picked up his leather carryall containing his tools and drove to the spot across from the apartment complex. He watched as the Mandels' car pulled past the guard booth out onto Cedar Road. He waited another fifteen minutes to make sure they did not return for some reason.

The coast clear, Bill put on a gray fedora and tipped the brim down to shield his face from security cameras. He grabbed his carryall and climbed out of his van. He placed a single ignition key on the mat. That way if he needed to vacate the premises in a hurry, he would not have to fidget with his keys.

He admitted in his book that he was on edge that night—more so than usual. Guards at the gate carried weapons.

Staying out of the guardhouse view, he walked up the drive and stalled until a group of people came along. The wait was short. A taxi pulled up to the gate. Five young partiers spilled out of it and proceeded to the building. Bill blended in with them. He casually walked through the lobby and took the elevator to the top floor. The door to the roof was still unlocked.

On the roof, he looked down into the atrium. The apartment was dark. He sat and watched it for some time. No movement. No lights. He unwound the rope from his waist. Using a carabiner, he secured it to a nearby smokestack, slung the carryall across his body and, hand over hand, lowered himself into the atrium. Before picking the lock on the sliding glass door, he looked for a security company decal. He did not see one. He looked for telltale wires or a magnetic strip on the door. He saw none. He peered through the glass into the apartment looking for a red blinking light on a wall panel. Nothing resembled an alarm.

The lock on the sliding glass door was flimsy. Bill jimmied it and let himself in. He waited for a moment to see if an alarm would go off. No alarm. He stepped a few feet into the apartment. The apartment was huge and expensively decorated with so much art that it looked like a museum, Bill wrote.

While getting into the apartment, he had turned the scanner low so he could listen to his surroundings. Once he was inside, he turned it up. No police chatter. He went to the front door and slid the bolt in place. The bolt would give him time to get out the way he came in. No one could come in the apartment and surprise him. "I never wanted to confront anyone," Bill said in Ratner's interview. "I always left myself an escape route."

Bill found a large dressing room with plenty of drawers and cabinets. It was easy to find the jewelry box, since it was the only one with a lock on it. The lock was easy. In his book, he related how the diamonds, rubies and emeralds glittered. One diamond ring looked to be around fifteen carats, but it did not look to be top quality.

Bill loaded his carryall with the spoils, slid the drawer back in and relocked it. The longer it took for victims to realize they had been burgled, the better for him. So much gold weighted his carryall down, making the climb back up to the roof more difficult. He rewound the rope around his waist, then realized he had forgotten to unbolt the door. He was not about to go back to unlock it.

Bill checked the scanner. Quiet. He hoisted the bag up on his shoulder and went down the stairs rather than the elevator and waited in the stairwell.

When he heard people in the lobby, he strolled out with the carryall, averting his face from the security cameras. He went out the main door past the guard house to his own car. On the way home, he dropped the bag off at his friend's shop.

The next day, he retrieved the jewels and burglary tools. The huge ring was the first thing he put under his jeweler's loupe. It was a nineteen-carat fake. He spilled the rest of the jewelry out onto the workbench and went through it piece by piece. More fakes. A ten-carat diamond pin—fake. He wrote that he was relieved when he found there were enough real stones to make the caper worthwhile.

The Mandels sued Acacia on the Green's management for $1 million, alleging security was insufficient. Mandel and his wife had moved from Shaker Heights because their home there had been broken into three times. They felt Acacia on the Green with its guard house and security cameras provided a safer atmosphere. According to a December 1984 article in the *Plain Dealer*, the jury awarded the Mandels $400,000 and added $100,000 in interest.

Bill was never arrested or even questioned.

In November 1982, Phyllis Diller returned to Northeast Ohio to perform at the Carousel Dinner Theatre near Ravenna. Copying his earlier successes, Bill parked down the street and waited for her limousine to pull out of the Carousel's parking lot. He followed it a short distance to Bryn Mawr Street and into an apartment building parking lot a couple hundred yards from the corner.

After she was safely in her apartment, the limo left. Bill pulled into the parking lot next door and climbed out. A tour around the building where Diller was staying told him there were only four apartments. Lights were on in only one, so he figured that was hers. Several buildings were on the same side of the road, but there was an empty lot across the street.

Bill returned a few days later, wearing dark clothing and carrying binoculars. Unsure what time the limousine would pick up Diller for the theater, he took up a position in the empty lot and waited in the cold. It finally came around 7:30 p.m. He waited another half hour before going across to her apartment. With cold hands, he fidgeted with his lock picking tools and got into the building. He left the door ajar and went back across the street to cut the wires to the telephone junction box, preventing anyone from calling the police.

Back at the apartment building door, he stuck a pin in the cylinder of the lock and pulled the door shut behind him. That way no one could get

Phillis Diller's jewelry was stolen a second time when she performed at the Carousel. Pictured with entertainment writer Irv Korman. *Irv Korman's collection.*

in the building, but he could get out a window. A thin piece of celluloid defeated the lock.

Bill did not have to hunt for Diller's jewelry. It was spread out in plain sight. It took no time to grab. Her address book was close by, and he grabbed that, too. The whole operation took only a few minutes, and he was out. He tried to get the pin out of the building door lock, but it was stuck and he had to leave it.

On November 20, 1982, the *Plain Dealer* reported that jewelry and cash worth $65,000 had been taken in the burglary. The paper said Diller could not get in the front door and had to climb through a window to get into her apartment. The newspaper also said phone service was knocked out to three-quarters of Ravenna.

Bill was disappointed with the take but happy to have her address book. That was something he would live to regret.

By September 1984, Bill had been a fugitive from Fort Lauderdale police for five and a half years. He kept a low profile, grew a beard, used a friend's identification and stayed away from places where anyone might recognize him. It was a good five years for him and Fran. They lived in a secluded rented house in Moreland Hills next to Chagrin Falls outside of Cleveland for two of those years. They went to parties and participated in social

The Moreland Hills house Fran and Bill rented. *From the* Plain Dealer.

occasions where no one would know him. They also traveled, together and separately. Fran often visited one of her daughters in New York, and Bill snuck in and out of Florida and Georgia to see his children.

One day, Bill had an unsettling experience. While in the hardware store near home, he saw an old acquaintance shopping toward the back of the store. He did not think the man would recognize him, but he kept his back toward that part of the store, just in case. He quickly selected what he needed, paid and left.

When Bill got out in the parking lot, he saw the same man sitting in a car parked a few spaces down from Fran's Mercedes, which he was driving. The man appeared to be reading something. Just as Bill opened his car door, he noticed what the man was "reading." A sheet of sandpaper. Bill's instinct told him to walk away, but he knew that would look suspicious, so he climbed into the Mercedes. The man wrote down Bill's license plate number and called his friend, Arthur Krinski, who was an FBI special agent. After that, the FBI put a surveillance team pretending to be telephone repairmen among other things on the Mill Creek house.

On September 13, 1984, Bill and Francine left their house and headed for Cleveland Hopkins Airport. Francine was going to New York, and Bill was flying to Atlanta to meet one of his daughters, then driving to Florida to see his son. The lovers kissed goodbye at the terminal and separated to go to their planes.

Bill was in line to check in at the Delta desk when four FBI agents grabbed him from behind and spun him around. As he was hauled away in handcuffs, he saw more than twenty plainclothes agents stationed around the airport. Francine was allowed to board her plane.

The authorities searched Bill's luggage and told the *Plain Dealer* they found notebooks detailing his capers. In his book, Bill claimed he would not have been so foolish. He did not feel the need to write out where he had been or what he had stolen. They found a notebook where he had jotted reminders to himself having to do with money, a "safe place" and changing his appearance. He was carrying the false passport and driver's license with the social security number.

Two days after Bill's arrest, the FBI and Chagrin Falls police knocked on the door of the Mill Creek Lane house with a search warrant. Bill claimed there was no justification for a warrant because he was arrested for being a fugitive. Chagrin Falls police justified the search warrant for other burglary cases.

According to the *Plain Dealer*, they found jewelry in plastic bags, in boxes and in a motor oil can. In *Confessions of a Master Jewel Thief*, Bill and coauthor Gruenfeld wrote that there was a lot of jewelry; however, Francine claimed it was all hers and that she could prove it. Police confiscated it anyway.

They also found $99,000 in cash, a very small amount of cocaine and some newspaper clippings about the theft of Phyllis Diller's jewelry and the Mandel burglary. Worst of all, they found Phyllis Diller's address book. They told Francine she would not be charged if she told everything she knew about Bill. She refused. The whole search was videotaped.

Bill was held on a $2 million bond. Attorney Jack M. Levin attempted to get the bond lowered. Assistant District Attorney Blas E. Serrano countered by stating Bill was a flight risk and he was on probation for earlier charges in Florida. Bill told the judge he had come to Ohio because his mother was having a second breast removed and he stayed because he was worried about her. She later died. Judge William Mahon listened to the arguments but tended to agree with the prosecutor and ordered Bill held without bond.

Serrano later said items found during the search tied Bill to crimes in Ohio. But Francine said the jewelry was all heirlooms and belonged to her from her twenty-one-year marriage to Marc Loveman. One of the pieces, a diamond watch, was engraved with her grandmother's initials.

Francine was not wearing any jewelry when she appeared before the judge and pleaded innocent to drug charges (0.03 grams of cocaine), obstruction of justice for harboring a fugitive and theft. Mahon continued her bond on the provision that she stay away from Bill.

Looking up from behind tinted glasses, Francine claimed not to know anything about his background as a thief, and she never saw him commit any crimes. "I know there's a wonderful man I love and that I can't get to see him." She told the *Plain Dealer* that they stayed home a lot, made grapevine wreaths and grew tomatoes. She said they took long walks and watched birds. It was a new life for both of them.

Fran Loveman in court. *Marvin M. Greene, the* Plain Dealer.

Francine knew there were some problems. Maybe she did not want to know what those problems were. "I don't judge people by their past. I fell in love with the man I know now."

In a plea deal in January, Francine pleaded guilty to obstruction of justice and receiving stolen property (the address book) through her new attorney, Gordon S. Freidman. The drug charges were dropped.

During her sentencing hearing the next month, she withdrew her guilty plea before Common Pleas judge Terrence O'Donnell. Her lawyers made a motion for O'Donnell to remove himself from the case. Friedman and Harvey H. Starkoff claimed the judge was no longer impartial. They maintained that O'Donnell's wife saw the search tape as the judge viewed it in preparation of sentencing.

In March, Francine was joined in court by her father, her sister and her one daughter when she pleaded guilty to the obstruction charge and receiving stolen property. Judge Frances E. Sweeney sentenced her to complete two hundred hours of community work and two years of probation. Phyllis Diller told the probation department that Francine was "harmless" and deserved probation.

Bill spent three months in the Cuyahoga County jail while authorities decided whether they wanted to press charges for the false passport. His Florida attorneys, Ray Sandstrom and Fred Haddad, felt he stood a better chance in Florida. Although his ex-wife offered her house for bail in Broward County, it was denied.

Bill was sentenced to five years. He was released after three and a half years and returned to Francine's arms. The two remained together through the years.

At the end of the interview, Ratner asked him if it was all worth it.

Bill closed his eyes and grimaced. "You know, numerous people have asked me that." He took a moment to think as he looked down. "Monetarily? No. If I'd a stayed in the real estate business, I'd of done much better."

He looked back up at his interviewer. "It's a different life. It cost me a lot of money. A lot of heartache. A lot of time. A lot of freedom." He lamented losing his wife and family.

But would he do it again? After all, at the time of the interview he was sixty-three years old.

"I certainly wouldn't make the same mistakes again, but would I take the same chances?" He hesitated a moment, and then with a twinkle in his brown eyes and a sly smile showing his white, even teeth, he said, "I might."

9
THE END OF THE ROAD

Charles Arthur Floyd hated the nickname "Pretty Boy." He may have picked up that moniker from a Kansas City madam who became infatuated with his dark hair and gray eyes. "I want you for myself, pretty boy." His future girlfriend Beulah Baird also said he was a pretty boy. The name may have stuck because he was particular about his clothing and hair. Some of the neighbors thought he was vain. One of his first robberies was at a Kroger store in St. Louis. The paymaster there described him as a "pretty boy with apple cheeks."

Born in 1904 in Georgia but raised in Oklahoma, Floyd grew up running through the woods of Cookson Hills, a former hideout for the likes of Belle Starr, the Dalton Gang and others. His family and friends knew him as Charley or "Choc," for his love of Chocktaw Indian brew.

Floyd's first brush with the law came when he stole $350 in pennies from the post office. He married in 1924 and had a son shortly after. He was devoted to his family, but dirt farming was hard work for very little return. In 1925, he participated in the Kroger $12,000 payroll robbery. He was rewarded with five years in the Missouri State Penitentiary for that crime, and his wife divorced him. After that stint in prison, he was on his way to becoming one of the most hunted bank robbers in history. Crime historians still doubt the official account of his death or whether he was involved in the Kansas City Massacre.

One of the first bandits to carry a machine gun, Pretty Boy Floyd was deadly with guns, quick on the draw, a crack shot, with steely nerves and

Charles Arthur Floyd did not like to be called "Pretty Boy." *Author's collection.*

plenty of daring. And yet he could be gentlemanly toward women and generous toward the needy. To some he was a Robin Hood. To others, he was a cold-blooded killer.

Floyd is credited with somewhere between thirty and forty bank robberies and twelve murders. Most of his crimes were committed in his home state of Oklahoma and neighboring Missouri. In 1930, he wound his way east to Ohio, where on February 5 he, James Bradley (a.k.a. Bob Randall, a.k.a. Bert Walker), Bob Amos, Jack Atkins, Nathan King and one unknown held up the Farmers & Merchants Bank of Sylvania. It was his first bank heist.

According to the *Toledo News-Bee*, twelve employees and patrons were in the bank when the outlaws burst through the doors, waving guns. Floyd lined everyone up in the lobby and covered them while King emptied the cash drawers.

Immediately before the robbery, cashier John C. Iffland walked up front from his desk in the back by the vault to talk with Mr. and Mrs. Frank Patten, who had come to the bank to look at some papers. When Iffland saw the robbers, he acted quickly to set the vault's time lock, which was close to his hand. King pistol whipped Iffland and kicked him, but once the lock was set, it could not be opened. There were $20,000 and negotiable Liberty Bonds beyond the robbers' reach. They also missed seeing Mrs. Patten slip her valuable rings off her fingers and hide them in her mouth.

Floyd and his partners did not realize that the victims were lined up in a spot that was clearly visible from the filling station across the street. The owner of the station, E.G. Howard, was also the vice president of the bank, and he could see the victims through the window with their hands up.

Howard got on the phone and told the operator to sound the village fire alarm. When Floyd, King and their gang heard the siren, they broke into a run for their car. The alarm possibly saved Iffland's life. Howard grabbed a shotgun, dashed out into the street and opened fire. The only thing he hit was a nearby car.

The village constable, Ralph Van Glan, and his deputy, Harry Reis, gave chase in the fire truck but lost them at Secor Road and Central Avenue. They searched all night but failed to turn up any trace of the robbers.

A month later, Pretty Boy, Nathan King and Bert Walker were in Summit County, hiding out in a two-story house on Lodi Street in a sparsely settled neighborhood just east of Akron. The canary-yellow house was one of the first in a new development. Police would later dub it the Canary Cottage. The outlaws rented it from William and Bertha Gannon.

Around 1:30 a.m. on Saturday, March 8, 1930, Akron police officers Henry Michaels, Arthur Possehl and Sergeant Steve Kovach were raiding houses of prostitution along Kenmore Boulevard. Traffic patrolman Harlan F. Manes was also in the vicinity. The policemen saw a woman staggering down the street in the direction of a sedan parked at the curb. Walker and King were sitting in the car. Police stopped the woman and asked what she was doing. She said she was waiting for her friend Bertha Gannon. The officer told her to get off the street. She walked over to the sedan. Shortly after, Bertha Gannon came out of a vice house that she owned. It was one of the houses the police had intended to raid. She was obviously drunk. Both women went over to the car at the curb.

Walker, who had been drinking heavily, was behind the wheel. Being that close to cops plus the alcohol might have been the reason he pulled away from the curb and recklessly drove through the nearby intersection. He hit a car that was traveling through the light. Patrolman Manes went to investigate with Sergeant Kovach as his backup. Damage was slight, and no one was hurt.

Although Akron police had a tip from Furnace Street Mission's preacher, Bill Denton, that Floyd and his gang were in town, neither Manes nor Kovack knew the two men in the car were part of the gang that pulled the Sylvania bank job.

Manes told Walker to get out of the car. All at once, Walker shoved Manes and drew his .38. He shot Manes point-blank in the abdomen. The officer staggered and fell. Gunfire erupted from Michaels, Possehl and Kovach. King sprinted from the car. The women scattered. Walker was wounded, but he fled the scene.

Every available officer was put on the street looking for Walker. King and one of the women, most likely Gannon, were nabbed. Both were tight-lipped when questioned at the station; they were not talking. One of the interrogators noticed that the soles of Gannon's shoes were covered in red dirt. The only red dirt the detectives could think of was in a new development east of the city.

According to an April 1953 interview with Detective Patsy Pappano in the *Akron Beacon Journal*, he, with Detectives Edward J. McDonnell, J. Sherman

Gandee, Louis Gustaevel, Bruce Ward, Gilbert Mosely, Denny Murray, Earnest Binkley, Cletus O'Farrell and Captain Steve McGowan put on bulletproof vests, armed themselves with shotguns, machine guns and tear gas and sped over the roads to the new development. They arrived at 5:45 that Saturday evening.

The house stuck out right away because of its color. On March 10, 1930, the *Akron Beacon Journal* described the raid. The article said that four detectives banged on the front door. The others surrounded the house to prevent anyone from escaping. The door was locked, so McDonnell kicked it in.

"Where are they?" he yelled at Nellie Denny, who met them inside. She pointed to the second floor. Guns drawn, six of the detectives charged up the stairs. One of the bedroom doors was locked. Pappano threw his weight against it. It splintered into pieces. They found Walker wrapped in a bloody blanket, lying in bed. Pretty Boy Floyd—or who they thought was Frank Mitchell—was hiding under the bed. Neither was armed, and they gave no resistance.

A search of the house turned up a small arsenal, containing a machine gun with a 150-round clip, a suitcase full of .45s, nitroglycerin and rubber gloves. Three car license plates turned up in the house. One of them matched the plate number on the car that sped away from the Sylvania bank robbery.

Right before Patrolman Manes died the next day, he tentatively identified Walker as the shooter. Walker was tried, and ballistics helped to convict him of murder. He died in the electric chair at the Ohio State Penitentiary in November 1930. Reverend Denton was with him. His last words were "I'm in for a shocking night tonight." He had also told lawmen, "If you think I'm tough, just wait until you have to deal with Floyd."

Floyd and King were sent to Toledo to stand trial for bank robbery. Floyd was booked as Frank Mitchell, alias Pretty Boy Smith. Bank employees identified Floyd and King as two of the robbers. They were convicted on November 24, 1930. Right before Floyd was to be sentenced, he made a break from the Lucas County jail. He and King had been permitted to go to the barber. As Deputy Chet Allen was bringing them back to their cells, Floyd used the other prisoners as cover and slipped out the side door. Allen saw him and quickly gave chase. Floyd ran out into heavy traffic on Michigan Street. His freedom was short-lived, as two police officers, plus Allen and Deputy Joe Packo, jumped him. He was hauled back to court and sentenced to twelve to fourteen years at the Ohio State Penitentiary.

Floyd had sworn to his pal King that he would rather die than go back to prison, but on December 10, 1930, he, King and a third prisoner, Ralph

Ball, boarded a train bound for the Ohio State Penitentiary. They were guarded by Packo and Joe Danielak. As usual, Floyd was well dressed but seemed resigned to what was ahead.

What Packo and Danielak did not know was that someone had slipped a handcuff key to Floyd, and it was under his tongue. It was a trick he had learned from fellow prisoner Willis Miller, a.k.a. Billy "the Killer." He also had a plan. He was going to imitate an escape he had read about as a child—that of killer Eddie Adams.

Once the train was under way. Floyd, who was handcuffed to King, asked to use the bathroom. The deputies denied him, but he asked several more times. When the train stopped at Kenton, he asked again. The deputies relented after the train started up. When Floyd and King went down the hall to the bathroom, Danielak went with them. In spite of having to leave the door open, Floyd managed to get out of the handcuffs, break out the window and leap to freedom.

Pretty Boy Floyd was on the run for the next four years. During those years, his rap sheet got longer and longer. He even partnered up with John Dillinger and maybe Alvin Karpis at different times.

Legend has it that he gave money for groceries and rent to needy families. Thinking he could release people from burdensome debt, he stole mortgage papers and tore them up during bank robberies. In return, people hid him from the law. A couple of sources claim he held up so many banks in Oklahoma that bank insurance rates doubled.

In April 1931, Floyd and Billy the Killer knocked over a bank in Whitehouse, Ohio, for $1,600.

Ballistics confirmed he was responsible for the deaths of William and Wallace Ash, brothers who were dope dealers and pimps. Worst of all, they were police informants. They were married to sisters Rose and Juanita Beulah Baird. The women then became his traveling companions. Beulah became his girlfriend.

Floyd and his gang killed a total of ten lawmen during shootouts and are blamed for the deaths of an FBI agent and three police officers at the Union Train Station during what became known as the Kansas City Massacre on June 17, 1933. Supposedly, Floyd, Adam C. Richetti and Vernon C. Miller tried to free federal prisoner Frank Nash, but Nash died during the shootout. Floyd always claimed that he was not there. An entry in Oklahoma Historical Society's *Encyclopedia of Oklahoma History and Culture* suggests that neither Floyd nor Richetti were involved. Witnesses to the carnage were shown photos of different suspects, but they passed by Floyd's. It was the one crime Floyd always denied. He even sent the governor of the state a postcard denying he had anything to do with the crime.

Floyd and Richetti retreated to Buffalo, New York, and stayed for a year. Rose and Beulah were with them. They rented apartments under false names as married couples. In October 1934, they decided to go home to the Oklahoma hills. Floyd had dreams of riding horses over the Mexican border and retiring. He and Richetti sent the women out to buy a car. They found a Ford V8 and paid $325 in cash.

They left Buffalo on October 18. The next day, they entered the Tiltonsville Peoples Bank in Tiltonsville, Jefferson County, Ohio, with rifles. Floyd and Richetti were later positively identified as being involved in the holdup. The take—Floyd's last—was only $500.

In the early hours of October 20, the foursome was driving in a dense fog outside Wellsville along the Ohio River. Richetti had a machine gun sitting across his lap. Floyd was driving. The conditions were bad, and he hit a telephone pole. No one was hurt, but the car needed repairs. The two men decided the women should take it into Wellsville to get it fixed. Floyd and Richetti removed the firearms from the car, took pillows, blankets and their coats and spread out on a hillside on the outskirts of town.

Locals Joe Fryman and his son-in-law, David O'Hanlon, were on the road right after dawn when they spotted Floyd and Richetti. Two men dressed in suits and sitting on a blanket on the hillside was a strange sight. Fryman, not knowing who the men were, was curious and went to talk to them. They told him they were taking pictures, but Fryman saw no camera. He thought it was fishy, so he, O'Hanlon and a local farmer, Lon Israel, called Wellsville police chief John H. Fultz. The chief wondered if the two strangers might have been involved in the Tiltonsville bank robbery the day before, so he and two officers went to investigate. He had his .38, but the other two were unarmed.

The chief found the two men. Floyd pulled his .45. Not knowing who he was dealing with, Fultz tried to talk with Floyd. A gun battle between Floyd and Fultz ensued. Fultz received a minor wound to his ankle. Floyd grabbed the machine gun, but its grip broke. He threw it down and took off up the hill through the brush and into the woods. The unarmed men ran to Israel's farm for shotguns. Richetti fled with Fultz on his heels and finally surrendered when he feared being shot.

Floyd ran through the woods where he was most comfortable. After a bit he came upon a farm where three young men were working on their cars. He asked if one would drive him to Youngstown. He said he would

Part of the Wellsville posse organized to hunt Floyd. *New York World-Telegram and the Sun Newspaper Photograph Collection (Library of Congress).*

pay them. Two of the young men were not interested, but eighteen-year-old George MacMillen needed the money and did not know who Floyd was. Floyd gave him ten dollars. During the ride, Floyd revealed his identity and showed him his gun.

MacMillen became afraid and pretended his car was running out of gas. Floyd spotted a Studebaker, a bigger, faster car. It belonged to sixty-year-old Wellsville florist James H. Baum. Floyd pulled his gun and forced both Baum and MacMillen into the Studebaker.

Tracking Floyd, Fultz came upon the young men on the farm and learned that MacMillen had driven away with Floyd in his Ford. He phoned the Lisbon sheriff's office and requested roadblocks for an unidentified fleeing suspect in a shooting. He told them he was looking for a Ford. Deputy George Hayes and Lisbon police officer Charles Patterson set up a roadblock on Ohio 45. In 1974, Hayes told *Akron Beacon Journal* reporter Peter Geiger that they saw a suspicious black car coming down the road, but it was a Studebaker, not a Ford. "After it came into sight, it turned into a driveway and backed out the way it had come. I turned to Patterson and said 'Charlie better follow that one.'"

They chased the car for several miles until it slid to a stop. Suddenly, a man broke out the glass in the back and began firing at the cops. Hayes's cruiser was riddled with bullet holes. One of the holes was right where Hayes's forehead had been. If he had not ducked, he would have been killed.

Floyd sprang from the car, bullets whizzing. The cops returned fire, but Floyd made it into the woods. Neither police officer was hit, but Baum was shot in the foot.

Police organized an armed one-hundred-man posse, but Floyd had a head start and was in his element.

At the Wellsville police station, Richetti was not talking except to say that he had not seen Floyd in a year. He said the man he was with was James Warren. Fultz sent Richetti's fingerprints to the FBI. The results came back quickly with Richetti's name and that he was a known associate of Pretty Boy Floyd. Now law enforcement knew who they were dealing with.

Melvin Purvis and three other FBI agents were in Cincinnati working a kidnapping case. When Purvis heard that Floyd was being hunted only four hours away, he called J. Edgar Hoover and asked for permission to go to Wellsville. Hoover agreed. Purvis kept in constant contact with Hoover during the hunt and was under extreme pressure to catch Floyd. More agents from Chicago, Cleveland, Cincinnati, Detroit, Indianapolis, St. Louis and Pittsburgh flooded the area and joined the hunt. Police up and down the eastern border of Ohio were on high alert.

Jeffrey S. King described the hunt for Floyd in his book *The Life and Death of Pretty Boy Floyd*. Squads of agents patrolled the roads in the area where Floyd disappeared. One squad raided the home of Richetti's half brother who lived forty miles south in Dillonvale. Convinced that Floyd had been wounded, agents talked with doctors and went to hospitals and clinics. Since Floyd always took to the woods during escapes, Purvis hired a pilot to fly a plane low over Spencer Woods, where there was a sighting.

By October 22, 1934, Floyd had eaten nothing but fruit from the trees for the two days he had been on the run. He stumbled out of the woods at Robert Robinson's farmhouse near the Bell Schoolhouse. He had walked eight miles in those two days. Robinson did not recognize the disheveled, unshaven man with red, scratched-up hands. He was suspicious of him nonetheless.

Floyd offered a dollar for something to eat. Robinson's daughter let him wash up and fixed him a sandwich, gave him ginger cookies and two apples.

He asked if someone would drive him to Youngstown, but the Robinsons refused. Then he asked for directions.

Floyd left then, and as he walked down the street, Robert Robinson watched him and realized who he was. Constable Birch drove by awhile later, and Robinson flagged him down. He told the constable about feeding Floyd, so the two drove six miles until they found FBI agents at a gas station.

The agents immediately called Purvis, who was manning the phones and taking reports from his agents in the field. He learned that Floyd was headed toward Youngstown. Purvis had heard that the outlaw had a girlfriend there, so he called Youngstown police and told them to be vigilant.

FBI agents joined forces with four East Liverpool policemen: Chief Hugh J. McDermont, Herman H. Roth, Chester C. Smith and Glenn G. Montgomery. The locals knew the area and got tips on sightings from area people. The combined lawmen drove the roads in two cars, stopping at each farm for information.

Barns, root cellars, abandoned buildings and sheds were searched. They took a few minutes to rest and eat some fresh fruit at one farmhouse. Little did they know that Floyd was only three miles away at the Conkle farm, situated two miles south of Clarkson and seven miles northeast of East Liverpool. It would be the FBI's next stop.

As the clock approached three that afternoon, widow Ellen Conkle, who lived alone on her farm on Spruceville Road, saw a stranger. "I was scrubbing the floor," she told the *Akron Beacon Journal Sunday Magazine*, "when I saw a man walking up the driveway. He didn't have a coat or hat and he was dirty. I stepped out to see what he wanted." Floyd approached her and said he was lost and hungry. He told her he had money and would pay her.

Apparently, Conkle did not read the paper, because she did not know who he was. She had no idea that there was a manhunt in the area and that the FBI was involved in it. But she must have wondered about his thistle-covered business suit, scuffed up oxfords and unshaven face. She even remarked that he did not have a hat. To explain his appearance, he claimed to have been squirrel hunting with his brother the night before and they had become separated.

"You don't hunt squirrels at night," she said, according to the DIGS archives from the *Pittsburgh Post-Gazette*.

After that he claimed that he had gotten drunk and become lost and did not know where he was. She did not believe that either. He did not look or smell as though he had been drinking. She thought he was jumpy. She became nervous when she saw the bulge of a gun under his jacket.

Conkle house where Floyd had his last meal. *James R. Dailey II's collection.*

Conkle asked him what he would like to eat. "Meat," he replied. All he had eaten was apples. She told him to go outside while she fixed his food, so he sat in the sun on her porch. After a while she told him to come inside, wash his hands and sit down to the table.

She served him what would be his last meal: pork chops, potatoes, rice, donuts, pumpkin pie and coffee. He told her it was a meal "fit for a king." He offered to pay her, but she refused. When he pulled a roll of bills from his pocket, she accepted one dollar.

Floyd had seen a Model A Ford parked by the corncrib and asked Conkle if she would drive him to Youngstown. She told him she could not. She said the car belonged to her brother, Stewart L. Dyke, and he might drive him part of the thirty-eight miles to Youngstown when he got back from the field.

Floyd went outside and got in the car to wait for Conkle's brother. After waiting a bit, he found the keys. He was getting ready to steal the car when Dyke and his wife walked up. Floyd asked Dyke to drive him to the bus line, but Dyke refused. He also refused to take Floyd to State 7 but finally agreed to drive him to Clarkson.

Dyke told his wife, Florence, to get in the back seat. She was uneasy about the man, but her husband said he would take care of it. He bid Floyd to sit in front with him.

Ellen Conkle showing the dishes that Floyd ate from. *James R. Dailey II's collection.*

Just as Dyke was pulling the car out, he saw two cars coming down the road. He said nothing. Floyd had not seen them. Florence Dyke did see them and remarked on the two cars.

Color drained from Floyd's face, and he went for his gun. He ordered Dyke to drive behind the corncrib. "They're looking for me," he said.

Dyke pulled the car behind the corncrib. He suddenly knew who he was dealing with. He bravely reached across the car and opened the door. "Get out, you son of a bitch."

"They're after me." Floyd jumped from the car and started to crawl under the corncrib, but there was only a twelve-inch space. He reconsidered. Hesitated. Looked to the woods, a familiar cover. Two hundred yards away. At first, he ran behind the garage.

Eight police and FBI pulled up and spilled out of their cars, yelling, "Halt! or we'll shoot!" and "Floyd! Come to the road or we'll shoot!"

Floyd burst out from behind the garage, running in a zigzag pattern, headed for the woods across the field of corn stubble. He was fast. He kept looking over his shoulder. His .45 was in his right hand, but he did not shoot.

Chief McDermott and Purvis yelled out, "Let him have it!"

Machine guns, shotguns, pistols and rifles rang out. Fifty bullets zinged through the air. Floyd ran a few more feet. His right arm jerked forward as a bullet hit his forearm. Searing lead tore into his body. He fought to go on, making it to a small incline, but then fell face-down. He rose up to his knees but dropped again and rolled over on his back.

There are two versions of Pretty Boy Floyd's final moments. The FBI files and Purvis's book claim that Purvis walked up to him and kicked his gun away. They examined him and found his second weapon, which was fixed to shoot fully automatic. "You're Pretty Boy Floyd," Purvis said.

"I'm Charles Arthur Floyd," Floyd answered. He was asked if he participated in the Kansas City Massacre. He denied it.

Purvis wrote in his book *American Agent* that he left the scene to call an ambulance and J. Edgar Hoover. There was no phone at the Conkle house. He claimed that he and another agent drove at "breakneck speed" to the next farm.

Another agent asked Floyd if he was one of the shooters at the Kansas City Massacre. Floyd answered with profanity. "I won't tell you nothing." Then he died.

Forty-five years after Floyd's death, retired East Liverpool police captain Chester C. Smith told a different story to *Time* magazine. At the age of eighty-four, Smith, who had been a sharpshooter, said he was the one who

Left: Melvin Purvis. *Author's collection.*

Below: The end of the road for Charles Arthur "Pretty Boy" Floyd. *Author's collection.*

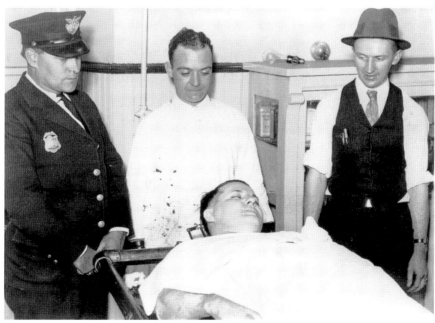

shot the two bullets that brought Floyd down. Smith was one of six police officers at the scene that day. Smith told the magazine, "I knew Purvis couldn't hit him, so I dropped him with two shots from my .32 Winchester rifle." Smith then disarmed Floyd. According to Smith's account, Purvis ran up to Floyd and told Smith to "back away from that man. I want to talk to him." Floyd cursed at Purvis. Purvis turned to Agent Herman Hollis and ordered, "Fire into him." Hollis obeyed the order with a burst from a tommy gun.

Retired deputy George Hayes told Geiger of the *Akron Beacon Journal Sunday Magazine* that other policemen who were there backed up Smith's version. In a letter to the editor of *TIME* titled "Setting the Record Straight," Winfred E. Horton claimed he knew Agent Hollis and that Hollis was not there that day.

Whoever shot him, Charles Arthur "Pretty Boy" Floyd died at 4:25 p.m., propped up against an apple tree with a soft breeze blowing.

Floyd's body was taken to Sturgis Funeral Parlors, where Drs. Roy C. Costello and Edward W. Miskall did an autopsy. The body had six fresh wounds that had been closed by stitches. "Due to the fact that the wounds had been sutured, at the time of examination it is impossible to distinguish wounds of entrance and exit." Death was by multiple gunshot wounds and massive internal hemorrhaging. The shooting was ruled justifiable.

The autopsy also said Floyd had a tattoo on his left forearm of a nurse with a rose. Curiously, the ends of his fingers had been smoothed by some abrasive substance.

Floyd was wearing a cameo ring on the fourth finger of his right hand. He was carrying $122 and change, a key, some matches, two apples and a loaded .45 clip. They also found in his pocket a Gruen pocket watch with a lucky silver half dollar attached to it. It had ten notches on it. Although he killed twelve people, it was thought the ten notches were for ten lawmen.

SOURCES

The People's Bandit

Books and Periodicals

Gorn, Elliott J. *Dillinger's Wild Ride: The Year That Made America's Public Enemy Number One.* New York: Oxford University Press, 2009.

Koile, Wendy. *Legends and Lost Treasure of Northern Ohio.* Charleston, SC: The History Press, 2014.

Meyer, David, Elise Meyers Walker and James Dailey II. *Inside the Ohio Penitentiary.* Charleston, SC: The History Press, 2013.

Poulson, Ellen, and Lori Hyde. *Chasing Dillinger.* Jefferson, NC: Exposit, 2018.

Toland, John. *The Dillinger Days.* New York: Random House, 1963.

Newspapers

Akron Beacon Journal
Associated Press
Canton Repository
Cincinnati Enquirer
Cleveland Plain Dealer
Dayton Daily News
Dayton Herald

Evening Review (East Liverpool, OH)
Kenosha (WI) Evening News
Kokomo (IN) Tribune
Marion Star
Marysville Journal
Newark (OH) Advocate
News-Journal (Mansfield, OH)
News Messenger (Fremont, OH)
Oshkosh (WI) Northwestern
Palladium-Item (Richmond, IN)
Piqua Daily Call
Richmond (IN) Item
Sandusky Register
Zanesville Signal

Websites

Andrews, Evan. "10 Things You May Not Know About John Dillinger." www.history.com.

Bluffton 1861. "Significant Events." www.bluffton-ohio.com/significant-events.

Bluffton Public Library Digital Archive. "Town at the Fork of the Rileys Revisited: Historical Sketches of Old Shannon and Bluffton, Ohio." https://ohiomemory.org.

Citizens National Bank. "History." www.cnbohio.com/resources/history.

Faded Glory: Dusty Roads of an FBI Era. historicalgmen.squarespace.com.

FBI. "John Dillinger." https://www.fbi.gov/history/famous-cases/john-dillinger.

———. "John Dillinger." https://vault.fbi.gov/John%20Dillinger%20.

Fox, Josh. "10 Famous Depression-era Bank Robbers." Listverse. listverse.com.

How to Be Your Own Detective. "John Dillinger Robbed Here First!" https://howtobeyourowndetective.com.

New Carlisle News. "The Life and Times of John Dillinger." www.newcarlislenews.net.

Reynolds, Bryan. "Ohio Native Recalls John Dillinger's Robbery in Bluffton." https://apnews.com.

Southard, Janie. "St. Marys Tied to Dillinger Gang." Daily Standard Story Archive. www.dailystandard.com.

THE CONRAD CAPER

Books

Renner, James. "The Ted Conrad Affair." In *The Serial Killer's Apprentice.* Cleveland, OH: Grey & Company Publishers, 2008.

Newspapers

Akron Beacon Journal
Bellingham (WA) Herald
Oregonian (Portland, OR)
Plain Dealer (Cleveland, OH)
Record Courier (Ravenna, OH)
Sacramento (CA) Bee

Websites

Ancestry.com.

City-Data Forum. "Theodore Conrad, Bank Robber." http://www.city-data.com.

Cleveland.com. "Theodore Conrad, the FBI Has a Long Memory. 39 Years Long." https://www.cleveland.com.

CoolInterestingStuff.com, "The Strange and Unsolved Ted Conrad Bank Heist." https://coolinterestingstuff.com.

Renner, James. *Lake Erie's Coldest Cases.* "Ted Conrad's Bank Heist." Investigation Discovery. https://www.facebook.com/watch/?v=1111755238985409.

Genealogy Bank. www.genealogybank.com.

ID Crimefeed. "Fugitive Bank Teller Ted Conrad Vanished with $215,000 50 Years Ago." www.investigationdiscovery.com.

KITV Island News. "Cleveland, OH Bank Robber in Hawaii after 48 Years?" https://www.kitv.com.

News 5 Cleveland. "Cleveland Federal Agents Continue Search for 1969 Bank Heist Fugitive Theodore John Conrad and $215k." www.news5cleveland.com.

Newspapers.com.

Ohio Mysteries. "1969: Bank Heist—The Ted Conrad Story." www.ohiomysteries.com.

Reddit. "On the Hunt: Theodore John Conrad." https://www.reddit.com/r/UnresolvedMysteries/comments/5u2abm/on_the_hunt_theodore_john_conrad.

Unsolved Mysteries of the World. "Where Is Ted Conrad?" https://shows.pippa.io/unsolved-mysteries-of-the-world/episodes/where-is-ted-conrad

YouTube. "The Ted Conrad Affair." https://www.youtube.com/watch?v=gT6zGSR35bo.

Looting the Library

Books and Periodicals

Eberhart, George M. "Kenyon College Wins $1-Million Theft Judgment." *American Libraries*, June/July 2003.

Hutt, Sherry, and David Tarler, eds. *Yearbook of Cultural Property Law*. New York: Routledge, 2016.

Ketchum, Robbie. "Kenyon Wins Suit." *Kenyon Collegian*, February 2003.

McDade, Travis. *Disappearing Ink*. New York: Diversion Books, 2015.

———. "The Unseen Theft of America's Literary History: There Are Thieves in the Archives, and We Don't Even Know It." *Literary Hub*, October 8, 2015.

Pitz, Marylynne. "Money Often Motivates Thieves to Purloin Papers, Botanical Prints, Maps, Atlases and Rare Books." *Pittsburg Post-Gazette*, July 20, 2018.

Saux, Frances. "Tale of Kenyon Archives Thefts Lives on in New Book." *Kenyon Collegian*, October 2015.

Court Cases

Kenyon College vs. Breithaupt, David and Hupp, Christa. Docket, case no.01OT 07-0211, Knox County Common Pleas Ct. (2001).

Newspapers

Cincinnati Enquirer
Columbus Dispatch
Daily Item (Sunburry, PA)

Newark Advocate
News-Journal (Mansfield, OH)
Pantagraph (Bloomington, IL)
Reporter Times (Martinsville, IN)

Websites

Ancestry.com.
Kenyon Review. "A Brief History of The Kenyon Review." https://
    kenyonreview.org.
Stillman, Michael. "The Worst Kind of Library Theft." Rare Book Hub.
    www.rarebookhub.com.

WHO WAS COWBOY HILL?

Books

Bailey, David. *Doctors Lawyers Swindlers Thieves: Gerald Chapman and the Tale of Two Gangs.* Muncie, IN: DSCBaileyBooks, 2019.

Newspapers

Akron Beacon Journal
Akron Evening Times
Ann Arbor (MI) News
Buffalo (NY) Evening News
Buffalo (NY) Times
Canton Repository
Cincinnati Enquirer
Cincinnati Post
Cleveland Leader
Columbus Dispatch
Daily Telegram (Adrian, MI)
Daily Times (Davenport, IA)
Dayton Daily News
Dayton Herald
Delta (OH) Atlas
Dispatch (Moline, IL)

Evening Independent (Mansfield, OH)
Fulton County Tribune (Wauseon, OH)
Grand Rapids (MI) Press
Plain Dealer (Cleveland, OH)
Quad City Times (Moline, Rockport, IL, Davenport, Bettendorf, IA)
Rock Island (IL) Argus
Sandusky Register
Toledo Blade

Websites and Historical Records

Ancestry.com.
Certificate of Death for Joseph Muzzio, October 17, 1937, No.63958, State of Ohio, Dept. of Health, Div. of Vital Statistics.
FamilySearch.org.
State of Ohio Penitentiary, Register of Prisoners with Index, Vols. 31–32, 1928–1933.
State of Ohio Penitentiary, Register of Prisoners with Index, Vols. 31-32, 1928-1933.
Toledo Police Museum. toledopolicemuseum.com.
United States Census, 1910, 1930.

CAUGHT ON CAMERA

Newspapers

Cleveland Plain Dealer
Cleveland Scene
Evansville (IN) Press

Websites and Historical Records

Cleveland.com.
Cleveland Police Museum.
DailyMail.com.
Death Certificate for Steven Ray Thomas, December 20, 1967, File No. '67 043702, Coroner's Certificate of Death, Indiana State Board of Health.

Record of Marriage. Steven Ray Thomas to Mary Katherine Shafer, January 19, 1963, File No. '63, Grant County, Indiana.

Record of Marriage. Steven Ray Thomas to Ruth Edna Taylor, November 20, 1964, File No. '64 001166, Grant County, Indiana.

Karpis's Mail Truck and Train Robberies

Books

Hoover, J. Edgar. *Persons in Hiding*. Boston: Little, Brown and Co., 1938.

Karpis, Alvin, and Bill Trent. *The Alvin Karpis Story*. New York: Coward, McCann & Geoghegan, 1971.

Koile, Wendy. *Legends and Lost Treasure of Northern Ohio*. Charleston, SC: The History Press, 2014.

Livesey, Robert. *On the Rock: Alvin Karpis, Public Enemy Number One*. Oakville, ONT, CA: Little Brick Schoolhouse, 2008.

Smith, W.D. *The Barker-Karpis Gang: An American Crime Family*. Amazon, 2016.

Turzillo, Jane Ann. *Murder & Mayhem on Ohio's Rails*. Charleston, SC: The History Press, 2014.

Newspapers

Akron Beacon Journal
Canton Repository
Chicago Sun Times
Cleveland Plain Dealer
Cleveland Press
Dayton Daily News
Minneapolis Star
Morning Star (Rockford, IL)
Seattle Sunday Times
St. Cloud (MN) Times

Websites, Interviews, Documentaries and YouTube Videos

Alcatraz History. AlcatrazHistory.com.

"Alvin Karpis Documentary from Discovery Channel." Part 1. From the series *Outlaws & Lawmen* 1996. YouTube video, June 20, 2008. https://www.youtube.com/watch?v=wn0xeqjwRC0.

———. Part 2. https://www.youtube.com/watch?v=BiN53f7VGLI.

"Alvin Karpis Interview!" YouTube video, April 11, 2015. https://www.youtube.com/watch?v=qv9F1pQja3U.

"Alvin Karpis 'Public Enemy No. 1.'" YouTube video, September 1, 2011. https://www.youtube.com/watch?v=HX--pkpsvBE&lc=UghkzqjE7sFl1ngCoAEC

Ancestry.com.

Faded Glory: Dusty Roads of an FBI Era. historicalgmen.squarespace.com

FBI. "The Alvin Karpis Capture." www.fbi.gov.

———. "Barker/Karpis Gang." www.fbi.gov.

———. "Bremer Investigation Summary." www.vault.fbi.gov.

———. "Closing in on the Barker/Karpis Gang." www.fbi.gov.

Turzillo, Jane Ann. "Hot Springs Madam Harbored Public Enemy No. 1." *Dark Hearted Women*, September 2012, darkheartedwomen.wordpress.com.

GRAVE CONCERNS

Books and Periodicals

Drusus, Livius. "The Body-Snatching Horror of John Scott Harrison." *Mental Floss.* May 21, 2015.

Shoemaker, John V., ed. *The Medical Bulletin: A Monthly Journal of Medicine and Surgery* vol. 7. Philadelphia: F. A. Davis, Att'y, Publisher, 1885.

Shultz, Suzanne M. *Body Snatching: The Robbing of Graves for the Education of Physicians in Early Nineteenth Century America.* Jefferson, NC: McFarland & Co., 1992.

Newspapers

Cincinnati Commercial Tribune
Cincinnati Daily Gazette
Cincinnati Daily Star
Cincinnati Enquirer
Detroit Free Press
Findlay (OH) Jeffersonian
New York Herald
New York Tribune

Websites

Ancestry.com.

Familysearch.org.

Findagrave.com.

Levinson, David. "Body Snatching." Brittanica. www.britannica.com/topic/body-snatching.

Ohio History Connection. "Medical College of Ohio." http://ohiohistorycentral.org.

United States Census 1870, 1880.

ALL THAT GLITTERS

Books and Periodicals

Drexler, Madeline, and James Neff. "Osgood, My Tiara's Missing." Forbes, April 11, 2004.

————. "The Thief and the Socialite." *Plain Dealer*, January 6, 1985.

————. "To Love a Thief." *Fort Lauderdale News*, April 14, 1985.

Kennedy, Randy. "Hello! Say, Is That Bulgari?" *New York Times*. April 18, 2004.

Mason, Bill, with Lee Gruenfeld. *Confessions of a Master Jewel Thief.* New York: Villard, 2005.

Neff, James. "Good Girl Gone Bad?" *Plain Dealer*, October 31, 1984.

————. "Tarnished Gem?" *Plain Dealer*, September 28, 1984.

Whelan, Edward P. "The Lady and the Outlaw." *Cleveland Magazine*, January 1985.

Court Cases

Village of Chargrin Falls v. Loveman, case no. 51134. Court of Appeals of Ohio, Cuyahoga County (1986).

Newspapers

Cincinnati Enquirer

Cleveland Jewish News

Fort Lauderdale (FL) News.

News-Journal (Mansfield, OH)

Plain Dealer (Cleveland, OH)

Rutland (VT) Daily Herald
Sydney Morning Herald (Sydney, New South Wales, Australia)

Websites, Blogs, TV and YouTube Videos

Ancestry.com

Blitzer, Wolf. Transcript of Interview with Bill Mason and Lee Gruenfeld. CNN.com, Sept. 1, 2003.

Broward County (Fort Lauderdale, FL) Sheriff's Office Public Records Unit.

Confessions of a Master Jewel Thief. Documentary. Organized Crime Channel. CourtTV. TV14.

Encyclopedia.com. Mason, Bill 1940-. March 8, 2004.

Evidence: Greater Ministries International. "Bill and Fran." CNBC, updated Oct. 8 2012.

Familysearch.com.

Fox, Josh. "Top 10 Infamous Cat Burglars." Listverse (crime). June 14, 2014.

Ratner, Brett. "Interview with a Jewel Thief (Bill Mason)." After the Sunset DVD, 2003.

THE END OF THE ROAD

Books and Periodicals

"Eyewitness Tells How 'Pretty Boy' Came to His Death." *United Press International*, October 23, 1934.

Farris, David. "Next Stop for Pretty Boy? The Slammer." *Edmond Life and Leisure.* Oct 5, 2017.

Geiger, Peter. "The Pretty Boy Floyd Murder and Cover-up." *Akron Beacon Journal Sunday Magazine*, October 20, 1974, 7–12.

Ingram, Dale. "Family Plot: Pretty Boy Floyd Relative Recalls His Infamous Uncle." *Tulsa World*, October 18, 2009.

King, Jeffrey S. *The Life and Death of Pretty Boy Floyd.* Kent, OH: Kent State University Press, 1998.

"Nation Blasting a G-Man Myth." *TIME Magazine.* Archived from original 1979.

Souter, Gerry, and Janet Souter. *Guns of Outlaws: Weapons of the American Bad Man.* New York: Quarto Publishing Group, 2014.

Wallis, Michael. "Floyd, Charles Arthur." *The Encyclopedia of Oklahoma History and Culture*. Oklahoma Historical Society. https://www.okhistory.org/publications/enc/entry.php.

Newspapers

Akron (OH) Beacon Journal
Circleville (OH) Herald
Dayton (OH) Herald
Evening Review (East Liverpool, OH)
Marion (OH) Star
Marysville (OH) Journal-Tribune
Newark (OH) Advocate
News Journal (Mansfield, OH)
News Messenger (Fremont, OH)
Piqua (OH) Daily Call
Toledo (OH) News-Bee

Websites

Biography. "Charles 'Pretty Boy' Floyd." www.biography.com.
Carnegie Public Library. East Liverpool, Ohio. "Charles 'Pretty Boy' Floyd." www.carnegie.lib.oh.us.
The Digs. "The Death of Pretty Boy Floyd." https://newsinteractive.post-gazette.com.
East Liverpool Historical Society. "Autopsy of Charles 'Pretty Boy' Floyd." www.eastliverpoolhistoricalsociety.org.
Encyclopedia of Oklahoma History and Culture. "Floyd, Charles Arthur." https://www.okhistory.org/publications/encyclopediaonline
FBI. "Charles Arthur 'Pretty Boy' Floyd." https://vault.fbi.gov.
———. "Kansas City Massacre/'Pretty Boy' Floyd." https://fbi.gov.
I Am Charles Arthur Floyd. "East Liverpool Police Captain Chester C. Smith's Time Magazine Account." https://sites.google.com/site/imcharlesarthurfloyd/blasting-a-g-man-myth/.
———. "Robberies." https://sites.google.com/site/imcharlesarthurfloyd/robberies.
———. "Winfred E. Hopton's Account." https://sites.google.com/site/imcharlesarthurfloyd/winfred-e-hopton-s-account.

Latson, Jennifer. "Hero or Villain? Why Thousands Mourned a Bank Robber." *Time*, October 22, 2014. time.com.

The Outlaw Journals. "8 Miles and a Sandwich: Here Come the Feds." https://babyfacenelsonjournal.com/floyds-death-2.html.

Tattoo History A–Z. "Pretty Boy Floyd." https://tattooarchive.com.

INDEX

ABOUT THE AUTHOR

True-crime author Jane Ann Turzillo has been nominated twice for the Agatha for her books *Wicked Women of Ohio* (2018) and *Unsolved Murders & Disappearances in Northeast Ohio* (2016). She is also a National Federation of Press Women award winner for *Ohio Train Disasters* and others—all from The History Press and Arcadia Publishing. A full-time author and speaker, she concentrates on true crime and history. As one of the original owners of a large weekly newspaper, she covered police, fire and hard news. Before she turned to writing books, she wrote short stories and articles that were published in newspapers and magazines across the United States and Canada. She is a graduate of The University of Akron with degrees in criminal justice technology and mass-media communication. She is a member of National Federation of Press Women, Society of Professional Journalists, Mystery Writers of America and Sisters in Crime. Visit her website at www.janeannturzillo.com and read her blog at http://darkheartedwomen.wordpress.com.